GLOBAL HISTORY OF THE PRESENT

Series editor | Nicholas Guyatt

In the Global History of the Present series, historians address the upheavals in world history since 1989, as we have lurched from the Cold War to the War on Terror. Each book considers the unique story of an individual country or region, refuting grandiose claims of 'the end of history', and linking local narratives to international developments.

Lively and accessible, these books are ideal introductions to the contemporary politics and history of a diverse range of countries. By bringing a historical perspective to recent debates and events, from democracy and terrorism to nationalism and globalization, the series challenges assumptions about the past and the present.

Published

Thabit A. J. Abdullah, *Dictatorship, Imperialism and Chaos: Iraq since 1989*

Timothy Cheek, *Living with Freedom: China since 1989*

Alexander S. Dawson, *First World Dreams: Mexico since 1989*

Padraic Kenney, *The Burdens of Freedom: Eastern Europe since 1989*

Stephen Lovell, *Destination in Doubt: Russia since 1989*

Forthcoming

Alejandra Bronfman, *On the Move: The Caribbean since 1989*

James D. Le Sueur, *Between Terror and Democracy: Algeria since 1989*

Mark LeVine, *Impossible Peace: Israel/Palestine since 1989*

Hyung Gu Lynn, *Bipolar Orders: The Two Koreas since 1989*

Nivedita Menon and Aditya Nigam, *Power and Contestation: India since 1989*

Helena Pohlandt-McCormick, *What Have We Done? South Africa since 1989*

Nicholas Guyatt is assistant professor of history at Simon Fraser University in Canada.

About the author

Alexander S. Dawson is associate professor of Latin American history at Simon Fraser University, in British Columbia, Canada. His research has focused on Indian–State relations in Mexico, and on the impact of globalization in Mexico. His publications include *Indian and Nation in Revolutionary Mexico* (2004).

First World Dreams: Mexico since 1989

Alexander S. Dawson

Fernwood Publishing
NOVA SCOTIA

Zed Books
LONDON | NEW YORK

First World Dreams: Mexico since 1989 was first published in 2006

Published in Canada by Fernwood Publishing Ltd, 32 Oceanvista Lane, Site 2A, Box 5, Black Point, Nova Scotia BOJ 1BO

<www.fernwoodbooks.ca>

Published in the rest of the world by Zed Books Ltd, 7 Cynthia Street, London N1 9JF, UK and Room 400, 175 Fifth Avenue, New York, NY 10010, USA

<www.zedbooks.co.uk>

Copyright © Alexander S. Dawson, 2006

The right of Alexander S. Dawson to be identified as the author of this work has been asserted by him in accordance with the Copyright, Designs and Patents Act, 1988.

Cover designed by Andrew Corbett
Set in Arnhem and Futura Bold by Ewan Smith, London
Index: <ed.emery@britishlibrary.net>
Printed and bound in Malta by Gutenberg Press Ltd

Distributed in the USA exclusively by Palgrave Macmillan, a division of St Martin's Press, LLC, 175 Fifth Avenue, New York, NY 10010.

A catalogue record for this book is available from the British Library.
US CIP data are available from the Library of Congress.

Library and Archives Canada Cataloguing in Publication:
Dawson, Alexander S. (Alexander Scott), 1967-
    First World dreams : Mexico since 1989 / Alexander Dawson.
Includes bibliographical references and index.
ISBN 1-55266-206-3
    1. Mexico--History--1988-. 2. Mexico--Economic conditions--1982-1994.
3. Mexico--Economic conditions--1994-. 4. Globalization--Mexico.
5. Mexico--Politics and government--1988-. I. Title.
F1236.D39 2006   972.08'35   C2006-902640-8

ISBN   1 84277 660 6 | 978 1 84277 660 5 hb
ISBN   1 84277 661 4 | 978 1 84277 661 2 pb

Contents

Acknowledgments

It seems fitting to me that this book begins in 1989, the date of my first visit to Mexico. In ways both small and large, this narrative is the outcome of countless encounters I have had in Mexico since then; conversations in libraries, archives, private homes, on the metro, and in the street, in which Mexican friends, acquaintances, and strangers told me their views on Mexico's global age. I hope that the stories that fill the following pages in large part reflect the things I learned in these conversations. I also owe significant debts to my teachers north of the border, particularly Paul Gootenberg, Barbara Weinstein, Brooke Larson, and Christon Archer. Always pressing me to make my work relevant, they taught me to try to understand Mexico's present even as I rooted through the archives in search of the distant past.

It was Nicholas Guyatt's idea that I write this book, and I am most grateful for the opportunity. He also read the manuscript carefully, and offered numerous helpful suggestions. Alejandra Bronfman also provided critical insights and guidance throughout the process, and read every word with a thoughtful eye.

Maia Q. neither read nor offered any help in the preparation of this book, but deserves the greatest thanks of all.

1 | Why 1989?

When Europeans and North Americans talk about globalization, they tend to conjure up a series of familiar images. Proponents rhapsodize about the fall of the Berlin Wall, information flows that allow computer users in Omaha to call help technicians in Bangalore, and recent events like the Ukraine's Orange Revolution. These are images of globalization as a positive force for economic growth and democratic change, producing efficiency and transparency across the planet. By contrast, when critics speak of globalization they talk of turtles protesting the WTO in the "Battle of Seattle," during November 1999, or imagine Indonesian children toiling in brutal conditions to make footballs, running shoes, and Christmas toys, while corporate giants reap huge profits. This imagery renders globalization as the triumph of global capital, a world where unions, social welfare, and popular sovereignty have been sacrificed to business interests, and where inequality and the worst excesses of capitalism – on the wane for nearly a century – are again on the rise.

If we take for granted that both these positions are viable, the logical place to start a history of globalization might be with the end of the Cold War. Each of the phenomena described above is rooted in global transformations since 1989, when the United States emerged as the sole superpower. Moreover, the end of the Cold War produced three distinct types of openings that can explain the variety of experiences that characterize the global era. The first trend has been the ascendance of market economics as the only model for determining the allocation of financial and other resources. Market economics and free trade have in turn changed the way the global economy works, as businesses have moved away from vertically organized companies with centralized production and distribution networks, towards a more complex web of interdependent producers, distributors, and consumers. Firms and capital are much more mobile, and tend today to act as brokers – buying, distributing, and selling over a web of sites of production and consumption (García Canclini 1999).

The second development has been the expansion of liberal democratic ideals on a scale never seen before. The 1990s saw the emergence of more governments based in democratic principles than at any point in the past. In Latin America this transition was particularly striking, as countries like Chile, Argentina, Peru, and Brazil emerged from long dictatorships with new democracies; adopting new forms of government and economic models that underscored the First World dreams of their governing elites. Third, these two trends have been associated with new forms of political and social protest; movements and individuals that embrace new technologies and techniques to globalize their struggles in innovative and sometimes terrifying ways.

And yet the problem with using 1989 as a starting point for the history of globalization is that it tends to reinforce the impression that globalization is something that started in rich, Western, industrialized societies, and spread to other regions. As with other diffusionist theories of civilization, this risks reinforcing the view that globalization is a story in which the West acted on a passive world, and where the center remains in the West. Mexicans in particular find 1989 a curious place to begin the history of their global age. When asked about memorable dates in their recent past, they rarely mention 1989. Instead Mexicans recall 1968 (the year of the massacre at Tlatelolco), 1985 (the Mexico City earthquake), 1994 (the year, as Carlos Fuentes put it, of "living dangerously"), and 2000 (the year seven decades of one-party rule came to an end). For Mexicans these dates tell an often tragic story of their country's bumpy road to democracy, and of the structural and social transformations that accompanied that process. Not coincidentally, these dates also tell the story of Mexico's participation in the global era.

Since Mexicans tend to mark 1968 as a singularly important moment in the recent history of their nation, this seems like a reasonable place to begin this narrative. Moreover, if we choose 1968 instead of 1989 as our starting point, globalization in Mexico seems to be less determined by the end of the Cold War than by a series of other processes. As the students who marched into Tlate-lolco on October 2, 1968 could have told you, they were already living in a global community. During their lifetimes Mexico had become a largely urban society, millions of Mexicans had come to own radios or televisions, and the cultural, political, and intellectual currents pulsing through Berkeley, Washington Heights, and Paris were as close as the nearest news-stand. Systems of social control put in place a generation earlier were breaking down; more and more middle-class Mexicans were demanding a life like the one they had seen or heard about in western Europe or the United States. They wanted a free university education, more social spending, and democracy within the university and the nation as a whole.

Sadly, as students in Prague, and elsewhere, learned during 1968, it did not always matter that the whole world was watching. On October 2, as eight thousand people gathered in the plaza at Tlatelolco, government sharpshooters hidden in the public housing projects that surrounded the square opened fire on the assembled protesters. Official estimates of the dead were twenty, with twenty-five injured, and 2,360 were detained, but witnesses suggest that the dead numbered over three hundred. Immediately afterwards government censors sprang into action, and ensured that almost no news of the massacre was published in the press. After initial news reports indicated that government troops fired on the students, the story was quickly changed to tell of terrorist snipers firing on police, who returned fire in self-defense. Hundreds of the protesters were imprisoned and charged with murder. Televisa, the television monopoly, showed no footage and reported the government account of events word for word. Army tanks rolled onto the campus of the National University (UNAM) to squelch the ongoing protests, and government forces arrested thousands more in the ensuing months. The most unlucky were murdered, their bodies dumped in the ocean.

A generation later, these atrocities would be unimaginable.

Before the global age

The students who demanded democratic openings in 1968 confronted a long history of authoritarian rule. Formally Mexico was a democratic republic. In practice Mexico's ruling elites maintained control by relying on a carefully managed political patronage system (clientelism), periodic social spending, and the occasional use of violence. This logic was particularly important to the state that emerged after the 1910 Revolution, the massive popular revolt that left over a million Mexicans dead. Sometimes called "the perfect dictatorship," the new state that emerged in the 1920s was controlled by the Party of the Institutionalized Revolution (PRI), which remained in power for seven decades through a careful balancing of regional, popular, and elite interests. The PRI was defiantly nationalist in its rhetoric and symbolism, but ideologically heterodox, capable of embracing socialist and capitalist agendas simultaneously. These tensions were often embodied in Mexico's all-powerful president, who could be both father to the peasant or proletarian, and ally to the agro-businessman or industrialist.

The PRI worked through three principal sectors – peasant, worker, and popular[1] – whose organizations endeavored to manage both their friends and enemies in ways that would allow the party to remain in power with only a minimum of physical coercion. Though never democratic, these organizations provided social mobility, access to power, and a variety of other benefits. Peasants, for example, obtained nearly half of Mexico's cultivable land from the revolutionary state in a process that was managed by the National Peasant Confederation (CNC). Unions affiliated with the Confederation of Mexican Workers (CTM) enjoyed protection under Mexico's labor code, and saw regular wage increases and fringe benefits. As members of the National Confederation of Popular Organizations (CNOP), peddlers, artisans, middle-class merchants, and businessmen enjoyed subsidies and preferential treatment from the government. Peasant, labor, and popular leaders who openly opposed the PRI were sometimes jailed or killed, but more commonly the PRI simply tried to stifle dissent without violence, often by purchasing the quiescence of the opposition.

For much of its time in power, the PRI's economic record was almost as impressive as its ability to ensure political stability. Through a program that combined labor peace, a tightly regulated food policy, federal control of natural resources (oil was nationalized in 1938, and electricity is a federal monopoly), and a vast array of subsidies and regulations,[2] between 1940 and 1965 the PRI produced an average annual growth rate in GDP of 6.3 percent. During these years the peso remained relatively stable,[3] and the earnings gap between rich and poor narrowed, a trend that lasted from the 1940s until 1976. During these years the percentage of Mexicans living in poverty gradually fell, reaching its lowest levels in 1981.

Behind these figures was a major transformation in the structure of the Mexican economy. Mexican industry grew from around 18 percent of GDP to over 25 percent, surpassing agriculture in value.[4] This was Mexico's economic miracle, a phenomenon in which industrial development acted as the key to political and social stability. Federal policies subsidized both production and consumption, and aimed to produce a politically loyal urban working class through public housing, education, social security, and food subsidies that kept staple prices low.

At first rural producers were not hurt by these policies, because a complex web of policies provided credit and aid to the peasant farmers who produced grain and maize for the Mexican market. In the 1960s, however, federal officials decided to allow a long-term drop in domestic staple prices (especially maize), favoring urban consumers at the expense of rural producers. Large commercial ventures oriented to agricultural exports received new support from the government, while small producers lost access to credit, irrigation, and fertilizer. Millions of peasants lost access to land under this policy, and as they exited the market domestic maize and grain production was increasingly supplemented with imports from the US. By the early 1980s Mexico was importing about half of its consumption needs in grain.

Federal officials had long wanted to drive rural producers out of peasant agriculture and into the urban working class, but by the early 1970s the domestic economy simply could not absorb rural migrants. Mexico, which saw its population grow from 36 million in 1960 to 80 million in 1985, needed 1 million new jobs per year to meet the needs of a growing urban population, and Mexico's new industries proved incapable of meeting this need. In part this was due to the fact that economic policies tended to promote capital-intensive industries, where increases in production came from technology, and as a result industry did not generate enough employment for a growing population. By the early 1970s unemployment was officially pegged at 10 percent, though underemployment was close to 40 percent.

Mexico's industrial sector faced other problems. During the miracle sectors that produced intermediate goods (i.e. fuel and fabric) flourished, while industries making capital goods (technology and heavy machinery) did not. Lacking the ability to create more capital-intensive goods, sophisticated products, or capital goods, Mexico did not develop an integrated manufacturing economy. Instead, the PRI's economic program produced an economy in which industry was inefficient and heavily dependent on government subsidies. This was a rent-seeking economy, in which bureaucrats determined the allocation of resources by issuing permits, licenses, restrictions, subsidies, tax exemptions, and import permits (by the early 1970s there were 13,000 different classifications of import duties in Mexico).[5]

While in the short run these policies created the basis for Mexican industrial growth and greater income equality across the economy, over the long run these practices were not viable. Along with the positive benefits, they also produced unsustainable balance of payments deficits (owing in part to a continued need to import components and parts for Mexican industry), low productivity and quality in industry, and an overvalued peso. These problems could be ignored in the short run, but over time were destined to produce sluggish growth and fiscal crises in the government. Mineral (principally oil) and agricultural exports remained critical to subsidizing industrial development even into the 1970s, but could not perpetually cover the costs of industrial development as deficits ballooned and inflation undermined wages and profitability.

The crisis

The Mexican economy was already veering toward crisis in the mid-1960s. Mexico's trade deficit grew from $367 million in 1965 to almost $1 billion four years later. Confronted by long-term capital shortages, Mexican businesses increasingly borrowed from abroad, accumulating a foreign debt of $3.2 billion by 1970.[6] President Luis Echeverría probably staved off a crisis in the early 1970s by combining an increase in the repression of dissidents with heavy borrowing from international markets to pay for an expansion of social programs and the state sector (he increased the number of state-run firms from eighty-six to 740),[7] but his measures would only make Mexico's economic problems worse in the long run. Mexico's public debt grew from 2 to 7 percent of GDP during his presidency. Foreign borrowing assumed a critical role in financing the deficit, and by 1977 50 percent of public spending was financed through borrowing.

Growing debt and low productivity produced a number of critical problems in the early 1970s. Inflation surged from 3 percent in 1969 to 17 percent by 1975, and the current account deficit grew from less than $1 billion to $4.4 billion. During the Echeverría administration the foreign debt grew from $6.7 billion to $15.7 billion. Not surprisingly, each of these phenomena was also associated with rising unemployment and capital flight. Bowing to growing domestic pressure to reverse these trends, in late 1976 the government reduced spending. The peso was allowed to float freely on the international exchange market in August 1976 for the first time since 1954, and fell from 12.5 per dollar to 26.5 per dollar by October. The fall of the peso was accompanied by widespread land invasions by peasants in Sonora, Jalisco, and Durango, and armed rebellion in Guerrero, as the rural poor made their growing desperation known to the nation. Echeverría would appease some of the peasant activists with land redistributions,[8] but the relatively meager 1976 reforms promised to do little to stem an emerging national crisis.

It was around this time that Mexican and international financiers began hearing rumors that PEMEX, the government-owned national oil monopoly, was sitting on a vast untapped reserve of oil in the Gulf of Mexico. Confirming those rumors, in 1976 PEMEX announced proven oil reserves of 6.3 billion barrels. New discoveries would place the figure at 45.8 billion barrels by 1979. Declaring that he wanted to "sow the petroleum," President José López Portillo (1976–82) launched a massive increase in social spending, created the Mexican Food System (SAM), which was designed to provide all Mexicans with their basic daily nutritional needs, and budgeted at $4 billion in 1980. He planned to pay for these efforts with a massive increase in oil export earnings, which did indeed grow from $311 million to $14 billion between 1976 and 1981. As a result of this boom GDP grew at over 8 percent annually in this period.

And yet Mexico's debt grew at an even more astounding pace. Between 1977 and 1982 Mexico earned $48 billion from oil exports, but borrowed $40 billion from abroad. Middle-class Mexicans remember this as a moment when they believed that their national destiny was suddenly in the First World, and where it seemed that they could rely on oil exports to subsidize any number of social and economic development initiatives. More than a few also saw this as an unprecedented opportunity for personal enrichment. Rumors abounded suggesting that López Portillo's wealth had soared into the hundreds of millions of dollars, though he, like most high-level officials, would never face any real scrutiny for the misappropriation of funds. Mexico City's police chief, Arturo Durazo, was not so lucky, perhaps because his opulence was simply too great to hide or excuse. Supposedly living on a modest salary as police chief between 1976 and 1982, he managed to maintain three mansions in the Federal District, as well as a vacation home in Zihuatanejo. Durazo (known as El Negro) was most famous for the replica of Manhattan's Studio 54 disco which he built in one of his homes. Jailed in 1985, he ultimately served eight years in prison.[9]

Amid the excess, the López Portillo administration actually oversaw a worsening of Mexico's trade balance. Deficits of $2.1 billion in 1978 grew to $3.6 billion in 1979, and $3.2 billion in 1980 and 1981. Other signs were also troubling. Inflation jumped to 40 percent in the late 1970s and was 100 percent in 1982. At the height of the boom inflation reduced workers' purchasing power by 6.5 percent, and businesses not connected to the oil industry were crippled by rising costs and reduced demand.

In July 1981 the government announced that falling oil prices had created a $1.2 billion shortfall in government revenues, and Mexico's current account deficit grew to $10 billion. Investors (both foreign and domestic) quickly responded by pulling their money out of the country, leading to a major drop in the government's dollar reserves. López Portillo responded by eliminating the fixed exchange rate on the peso in February 1982. It fell to 45 pesos to the dollar before the government reimposed exchange controls. In August the peso was allowed to trade freely again, and within weeks was trading at 80 to the dollar.

It was then that the debt crisis that defined Mexican and more broadly Latin American experiences in the 1980s began to take shape. López Portillo suspended payments on the debt, and then nationalized the banks. He ordered that those Mexicans who held US-denominated dollar accounts convert their accounts to pesos at below market value (López Portillo claimed that private banks had plundered Mexico in the crisis). As their wealth evaporated businessmen and members of the middle class (25–30 percent of the urban population) faced devastation, especially if they had debts denominated in US dollars. They watched in outrage as López Portillo retired to a compound with five mansions, tennis courts, swimming pools, and horse stables on a hill in the western suburbs of Mexico City in December 1982.

Mexico's total foreign debt (public and private) grew from $48 billion in 1980 to $80 billion in 1982. By 1987 it would grow to $100 billion, and equal 70 percent of GDP. Oil exports offered little relief, as by 1982 almost half of foreign export earnings were needed to finance the debt. Not coincidentally, the number of Mexicans with money deposited abroad also skyrocketed. Mexicans sent $22 billion out of the country in the final two years of the López Portillo regime alone, and during the worst crisis years sent roughly $90 billion abroad. This tendency led one member of the US Federal Reserve Board to comment, in the middle of negotiations over the debt, that Mexico's problem was not a lack of assets, but that the assets are "all in Miami."

For those Mexicans who could not send money abroad, the six years of the Miguel de la Madrid regime (1982–88) produced the worst suffering they had seen in generations. Seeking to improve Mexico's creditworthiness in the eyes of the International Monetary Fund (IMF), in December 1982 de la Madrid introduced the first of a series of shock treatments designed to restore fiscal stability through dramatic cuts in spending and major peso devaluations. He inherited 1,115 public companies in 1982, and sold ninety-six, merged forty-six, and transferred thirty-nine to state governments by 1986. He shut down 279 inefficient plants, lifted price controls on 2,500 goods, introduced price flexibility to 2,000 more, and allowed the peso to float on the international market, where it fell to 150 to the dollar. He also immediately renegotiated the debt with the IMF, and agreed to reduce the budget deficit from 18 percent of GDP to 3.5 percent in 1985. One critical result was that discretionary spending (that is, spending unrelated to debt payments and other legally required outlays) fell from 80 percent of the budget to 54.3 percent between 1983 and 1988. Total government spending fell by 6.8 percent, and social spending fell by 33.1 percent.

Most of the burden fell on workers. The purchasing power of workers fell at 15–20 percent per year after 1982. The SAM was abandoned for a more modest program that spared the desperately poor, but raised food prices for working Mexicans. In an effort to open more land to large-scale production, de la Madrid reformed agricultural policy to remove excess labor from the countryside. He reduced financial supports to small farmers (the budget for the federal Ministry of Agriculture fell by 70 percent), and removed tariff barriers against cheap foreign foodstuffs.

Even these measures did not restore growth to the economy. Declining domestic demand drove the country into a deeper crisis and had little impact on inflation. Disappointed by de la Madrid's failure to produce growth, in September 1985 the IMF suspended disbursements on a loan it had negotiated in 1982 as a part of an agreement to resume payments on the debt. This led to a further run on the peso, a deeper economic crisis, and more austerity measures. Wages fell yet again, the credit squeeze intensified, and a number of experts began warning of levels of poverty, hunger, and disease in the countryside that had not been seen in decades.

By the mid-1980s many Mexicans bemoaned the fact that the blessings of oil had turned out to be a curse. Oil served as a powerful symbol of both hope and disaster (made more powerful because of the broadly acknowledged phenomenon of "oil sickness," whereby oil tends to distort developing economies over time), but the curse of oil alone does not explain the crisis that Mexico faced in 1982. More than just the result of falling oil prices, the crisis was also brought about by changes in global financial markets. In the late 1970s the cost of the debt rose owing to rising global interest rates and a weakening economy, and Mexicans, like their neighbors throughout Latin America, found themselves saddled with debt that left them more vulnerable to the demands of international credit agencies (particularly the IMF). Latin Americans needed help from the IMF and World Bank, but were forced to adopt their models of economic reform in order to find a sympathetic ear in First World economic institutions. All efforts to remind First World bankers and finance ministers that the debt was in part the result of their own lending practices, and that it represented a net transfer of wealth from poor to rich nations in a time of crisis, fell on deaf ears.

Yet the debt also offers only a partial explanation of the crisis. There were serious signs of trouble in the Mexican economy long before the oil boom and the expansion of the debt. Stagnant growth, a poor trade balance, inflation, and fiscal crisis had been features of the Mexican economy even in the late 1960s; the early signs of a crisis in the economic model that had produced the miracle. Most economists now conclude that oil simply put off a crisis that would otherwise have happened several years earlier, and then made that crisis more extreme. In turn, the response was also more extreme because after 1982 the foreign debt gave Mexican officials much less room to maneuver. Crippled by external constraints and internal crisis, the state simply no longer had the resources to pay for many of the programs Mexicans had come to expect. And as Mexicans would find out under tragic circumstances, that state was in such a deep crisis that it would prove unequal to the simple task of protecting the lives of its citizens.

September 19, 1985

On September 19, 1985, at 7:19 in the morning, an earthquake registering 8.1 on the Richter scale hit Mexico City. More than 370 buildings collapsed, including two public hospitals, and numerous public housing complexes. Constructed hastily and often structurally unsafe (in part due to the widespread practice of bribing building inspectors), public housing was particularly hard hit. Typical was the case of the Nuevo León, a building in the Tlatelolco complex collapsed, killing 472. Weeks before the earthquake the residents had placed a banner on the building decrying the federal housing agency's failure to make their building safe after an earlier earthquake. In response to their protest an agency engineer had declared that the building was one of the safest in Mexico City. The banner was found in the rubble.

In the hours after the earthquake, as perhaps 20,000 lay dead underneath the rubble and another 100,000 sought help for their injuries, emergency workers failed to materialize. People in affected urban housing projects saw their pleas to local authorities go unanswered. They had to dig out the injured and dead by themselves, using their hands and crude implements. Soldiers sent to the most devastated areas to protect buildings joined in the looting instead, or blocked volunteers from helping in the worst-affected areas. On the Calzada de San Antonio Abad, sweatshop owners did manage to hire heavy machinery to dig out their factories, but they used the machines to remove equipment and inventory, and did not make any efforts to find out who was in the buildings or rescue them. Because their mostly female workforce worked off the books, they could simply claim that none of their employees lay in the ruins. Some seamstresses remained in the rubble for days.

Federal officials responded to a growing wave of protests in a manner that only stoked growing public rage. They obstructed, refused to help, and at times even hindered rescue efforts. They told people to go home, be patient, and did not offer aid. Officials particularly distrusted volunteer efforts, insisting that the authorities were "in control." President de la Madrid remained mostly out of sight, and refused to approach the devastation when he toured damaged areas (some claimed he did not want to get his clothes dirty). It was only after a second quake on September 20 that he began to acknowledge the magnitude of the crisis, admitting that the state did not have the resources to deal with the situation. He asked Mexicans to be patient.[10]

Patience was a commodity that the victims did not possess, and they quickly formed a series of independent auxiliaries that simply bypassed the federal government. Protesters marched on Los Pinos (the presidential palace) a week after the earthquake. Marches were not uncommon in Mexico, but this was unusual. Unlike traditional PRI demonstrations, these groups were organized from the bottom up, and ignored political patronage networks. Deeply enraged by the corruption, incompetence, and lack of leadership they saw in the aftermath of the earthquake, the 180,000 people left homeless suddenly emerged as a new political force. Symbolized by the cartoon-like *Superbarrio* – a hero for the poor dressed in the elaborate costumes favored by Mexican wrestlers – the victims of the earthquake exposed the worst excesses of the Mexican political system.

Their protests were spurred on by an economic crisis that grew even more acute after the earthquake. During 1985 GDP fell by 3.4 percent. Then, in December, oil prices began falling for the second time in five years. Between December 1985 and July 1986 the price of oil fell from $23.70 per barrel to $8.90. This amounted to a loss of over $8 billion in foreign earnings, and during 1986 GDP declined by another 6.4 percent. By the start of 1987 the peso was trading at more than 1,000 to the dollar. It was 1,400 to the dollar by mid-year. Inflation during 1987 ran at over 100 percent.

Openings

Mexicans often mark the 1985 earthquake as the nadir of Mexico's lost decade. Perhaps not surprisingly, it is also often remembered as the moment when Mexico's political system began to change. To tell that story, however, we must return once more to 1968.

Almost a decade of social change and conflict came out into the open during the summer of 1968, and Tlatelolco was just one of many signs of an emerging political crisis. On August 27, five weeks before the massacre, 400,000 protesters marched in Mexico City's central plaza, the Zócalo. Army tanks rolled into the National Autonomous University (UNAM) on September 18 to quell a student strike that had crippled the campus. Students and young people throughout the country took part in the demonstrations, including a young Ernesto Zedillo, Mexico's future president, who protested as a sixteen-year-old after police attacked teachers and classmates inside his school, Vocational Number 5.

In the short run Tlatelolco gave way to a brief burst of violence in the countryside, where some of the more militant activists fled to foment revolution. Guerrilla movements in Guerrero under Lucio Cabañas managed to kidnap the state governor, but petered out by the mid-1970s as their leaders were captured and killed. Urban protest also waned, as federal security agencies became more adept at infiltrating, disrupting, and brutalizing subversives. Students marching in 1971 were attacked by a unit organized by Echeverría for such purposes, the Falcons (Halcones). Though they were disbanded and went into hiding immediately after the attacks, the very existence of the Halcones reminds us of a state that believed it could attack, silence, and imprison its citizens with impunity.

Imagined another way, the Halcones revealed a state that was increasingly aware that the traditional mechanisms of political and social control were beginning to break down. And the signs of this breakdown were everywhere. The events of 1968 shattered the benign image of the PRI, and while the party still controlled most of Mexico's erstwhile public spaces, small acts of dissent rattled the regime. It was not insignificant that Octavio Paz resigned as ambassador to India in the aftermath of Tlatelolco. His decision was a sign that Mexico's public intellectuals, long bought off with fancy appointments and generous stipends, were beginning to slip out of the revolutionary fold.

After 1968 a tradition of intellectual quiescence gave way as a new generation of public intellectuals openly challenged the PRI and its practices. In 1971 Elena Poniatowska's *La Noche de Tlatelolco* (translated as *Massacre in Mexico*) shocked the Mexican public with its graphic and tragic detail about the events of October 2, 1968. Poniatowska obliterated the official story in her account, estimating that 325 people had been killed in the massacre, and claiming that the bloody events were entirely the responsibility of government forces. After successfully keeping newspapers relatively free of accounts of the massacre for three years, federal officials were taken by surprise by the book. It went through several editions by the year's end.

Still, the Mexican press remained relatively subservient to the PRI. Mexican journalists have always been poorly paid, and consistently made up for their salary deficiencies by taking payments from public officials to write stories, favor certain positions in their stories, or ignore stories altogether. Many of the capital's newspapers were traditionally financed out of slush funds from the PRI. Perhaps two-thirds of the newspapers in the country survived by publishing *gacetillas*, news stories provided and paid for by the government. Reporters also received bribes, called *chayotes,* to write stories in favor of the government. Other perks included gifts, food, drinks, free travel, and prostitutes.

Federal officials also paid large sums to suppress stories. A type of soft compulsion, these payments often went all the way up to editors, and formed the basis of Mexican newspaper reports about the state. If a paper refused to publish stories provided by the state, or published something critical, they would find themselves suffering from paper shortages, struck by their various unions (which were invariably PRI-affiliated, dependent on federal largesse, and often used as political muscle), and perhaps physically threatened. Even at the most prestigious papers in the country, editors could be fired if they angered the party, and most chose to do whatever they needed to do to keep their jobs.

This began to change in the aftermath of Tlatelolco, when a growing number of reporters and intellectuals found that they could no longer play the old game. Paz returned to Mexico in 1971 to edit *Plural*, and in 1976 founded *Vuelta*, a literary magazine that acted as a critical forum for dissent. When Julio Scherer García was ousted from *Excelsior* (a leading daily) at Echeverría's request, he founded *Proceso* (1976), which became the center of political criticism in Mexico. *Nexos*, *Siempre*, and *Unomásuno* would follow shortly, revolutionizing the relationship between the press and the Mexican state. In the 1980s a series of daily newspapers, *Reforma*, *La Jornada*, and *El Universal* in the Federal District, and *Zeta* (Tijuana), *El Imparcial* (Hermosillo), and *Siglo 21* (Guadalajara) outside Mexico City, became critical sources of independent reporting. *La Jornada*'s creation in 1984 in particular proved particularly fortuitous for Mexicans. When de la Madrid ordered the local press to stop reporting the aftermath of the 1985 earthquake, *La Jornada* was the only paper that refused. Their stories about the earthquake exposed the PRI to more public scrutiny than it had ever seen.

By the late 1980s the proliferation of media made it increasingly difficult to suppress stories that cast the PRI in a negative light, so the PRI began to curtail its efforts to buy off the media. This further weakened the link between the print media and the state, as those papers that depended most heavily on the PRI faced financial ruin. The exception to this decline would be the TV networks, whose reliance on the state for licenses, monopolies over new technologies, and lucrative contracts to broadcast soccer would keep television in the pockets of the PRI into the late 1990s.

Even with a virtual PRI monopoly on TV, by the end of the 1970s it was increasingly easy for Mexicans to get news about their own country and the world by bypassing the state-dominated media. Mexicans could read newspapers and magazines published in the US (where reporting on events in Mexico was becoming more common), talk to relatives living abroad, and (after the mid-1980s) receive the latest gossip by fax machine. Fax machines had a particularly significant impact on the dissemination of information, given that mail delivery was inconsistent and phone service very expensive. Furthermore, a growing number of Mexicans of all classes found themselves living abroad during these years, some as students, some as executives, but most as migrant laborers. Many of the individuals who would later join the political opposition had their first taste of real oppositional politics as they traveled, studied, and worked abroad.

Sergio Aguayo (b. 1947) was one of these individuals. He supported the PRI while growing up in Guadalajara, but was transformed by the events of 1968. After participating in local student politics, Aguayo became a target of government repression in Guadalajara, and in 1971 he left for the relative anonymity of Mexico City. He later enrolled in the Colegio de México, and continued his education in the United States, where he received a PhD in International Relations from Johns Hopkins in 1984. Like thousands of Mexicans who went to US universities during this decade, he returned with new ideas about politics and democracy.

After his return to Mexico, Aguayo helped found SEDEPAC (Service, Development and Peace), one of a growing number of NGOs that appeared in Mexico during the 1980s. Aguayo devoted his spare time to promoting political activism throughout the country, from urban slums in Mexico City, to assembly plants on the northern border, to indigenous hamlets in Tlaxcala and Michoacán. SEDEPAC also worked with international organizations, including the American Friends Service Committee, organizing *maquila* (assembly plant) workers in the early 1980s. The early results were decidedly mixed.

Always, Aguayo reminded all those he tried to mobilize that they did in fact possess rights guaranteed by the Mexican constitution. Was this arrogant? Perhaps. Influenced by US civil rights movements? Indeed. Out of touch with Mexican political practices? Certainly. Describing an effort to organize Zenith employees in Matamoros during the mid-1980s, which prompted harsh government repression, he comments:

> In Matamoros, we raised consciousness, we encouraged their organization, and we stood by them when they moved. But neither the workers nor we had the lawyers, the money to survive, the media willing to inform objectively (any movement that is denied accurate press coverage is fundamentally challenged from the very start). Nothing like that existed in the Matamoros of 1984. Matamoros was a very hostile place for independent movements.

Even though Matamoros ended badly, Aguayo and a growing network used these experiences to refine their strategies. He organized groups to support Central American refugees and promote human rights. He began to speak more openly about the idea of universal rights, building organizations that crossed national boundaries. Opponents called him a sell-out for his close ties to North American organizations, but these ties created the support networks that he needed to monitor both human rights and Mexican elections. These organizations also helped his work as president of the Mexican Academy of Human Rights (1990–96), where he trained thousands of activists to monitor elections, human rights abuses, and the conditions under which poor Mexicans lived and worked.

Whether promoting voting rights, human rights, environmental conservation, women's rights, or any number of other concerns, the web of organizations that flourished in these years transformed civil society. No longer would the PRI be a center around which a pyramidal public life functioned. Whereas at one time organizations that challenged the PRI could work only on the local level, by the mid-1980s these NGOs reached across regions and international boundaries. Mexico's entry into global trade and other agreements would only enhance their power to remake both Mexican society and Mexican politics.

Political challenges

Aguayo and many other activists eschewed politics in favor of a struggle for civil and human rights, a decision that may in part have been informed by the chilling effect that 1968 had on open forms of opposition to the regime. Yet there were those who persisted in the political opposition. One of the most notable of these was the Coalition of Workers, Peasants and Students of the Isthmus (COCEI), organized in 1971 by a group of leftist Zapotec activists in Juchitán Oaxaca. Their struggles were particularly courageous, given the ways in which the PRI often held on to power in rural areas. Zapotec leaders protesting the loss of communal lands to development projects and the expansion of commercial agriculture were routinely murdered, though by the 1970s this practice had generated such deep-seated antipathy toward the PRI that the COCEI thrived in spite of the threats. After a decade spent organizing community members and making demands on behalf of the community, the COCEI somehow won the municipal elections in Juchitán in 1981. The victory was a surprise for everyone. No opposition party had held a municipal office in the country for several decades. Two years later the PRI forced COCEI from office in a fraudulent election that resulted in the torture and deaths of eighty-six COCEI supporters, but the COCEI managed to retake the municipal offices by forging an agreement with the local PRI in 1986.

The 1980s also saw the emergence of opposition parties on the national level. In 1977 López Portillo (who ran unopposed in 1976, winning 91.9 percent of the vote) agreed to political reforms that gave citizens the right to organize political parties, and guaranteed proportional representation in the legislature. In 1979 opposition parties won 104 seats in the 400-seat Chamber of Deputies. The National Action Party (PAN), a northern, business-friendly, and pro-Catholic party, was the biggest winner, securing forty-three seats.

Mexico's northern states have long been distinct from the rest of the country, and northerners sometimes distinguish themselves with the aphorism: "The North works, the Center thinks, and the South sleeps." As the saying suggests, northerners imagine themselves as a part of a frontier society, more connected to their neighbors just on the other side of the border than to other Mexicans. A long history of cross-border migration and territorial loss punctuates this sentiment, as many millions of northerners have family members on the other side of the border. They are "working people," businessmen with an entrepreneurial spirit, who have for the better part of a century resented the rest of the country as a burden on their resourcefulness. In the 1980s they also had more access than their southern countrymen to foreign media coverage of events in Mexico. As the most bilingual sector of the population, they could read American newspapers and talk to family members to gather news.

Because they relied on a dollar economy, northerners were particularly devastated by the bank nationalizations in 1982. In the ensuing crisis thousands of businesses were crushed, and millions of middle- and upper-class Mexicans lost their savings and assets. In turn, many northerners became convinced that the Mexican political system was altogether too corrupt, anti-democratic, and backward. The PAN was the predictable beneficiary of these developments. PAN candidates won the races for mayor of Chihuahua City and Juárez in 1983, prompting new efforts by the local PRI to win through electoral fraud. In the 1986 election for governor in Chihuahua, PRI activists stuffed the ballot boxes before the polls opened, disqualified poll watchers, and made up phony voter lists, producing a lopsided and obviously fraudulent PRI victory.

But 1983 was not 1968, and the PRI's shenanigans set off a round of violence and large-scale protests. Local protests eventually attracted the attention of national intellectuals, who in the following months exposed the full extent of the fraud in Chihuahua. Though the PRI held on to Chihuahua in 1986, by the time of the 1988 presidential election Mexicans were more mobilized than they had been in decades. The PAN was ascendant throughout the north, and ran businessman and farmer Manuel Clouthier de Rincón as its candidate. In central Mexico dissident *priistas* (PRI supporters) coalesced around Cuauthémoc Cárdenas Solórzano's umbrella organization, the National Democratic Front (FDN), which included several leftist parties. Cárdenas was a PRI insider, having relied on presidential power to become governor of Michoacán in 1980, but as governor he emerged as an advocate for democratic change and social justice. He was expelled from the PRI in 1987 after he accepted the presidential nomination of a small party.

Given the extent of the political and economic crisis, it seemed possible that Cárdenas might win the election. The final year of de la Madrid's tenure saw an inflation rate of 160 percent, the economy was in terrible shape, and the electoral and other scandals facing the PRI seemed overwhelming. On top of this, de la Madrid's hand-picked successor, Carlos Salinas de Gortari, seemed like a lackluster choice. Like de la Madrid, Salinas was a Harvard graduate who came from the ranks of PRI technocrats, and had never even held an elected office. By contrast, Cárdenas was the son of perhaps Mexico's most popular revolutionary president, and gathered huge crowds wherever he traveled during the election.

Most of the PRI's internal polls showed Salinas winning by a small margin, but this did not mollify their concerns. In the weeks leading up to the election the press intensified its attacks on Cárdenas, and someone in the PRI went so far as to kill Cárdenas's chief pollster. The murder left Cárdenas unable to collect accurate polling data, ensuring that it would be hard to produce the evidence needed to contest a close election.

Standard PRI practices came out in force on election day. Voters found boxes filled before their polling stations opened, many polling stations never opened, and in other places boxes were stolen by armed thugs. Voting lists were manipulated, often allowing *priistas* to vote several times in different places. Local election committees inflated Salinas's numbers by adding zeros to his vote total in thousands of precincts. When opposition poll watchers protested, PRI-dominated local committees voted to approve the decision to inflate the vote totals, and opponents were asked to respect the democratic process. The Federal Elections Commission, controlled by the PRI, simply rubber-stamped these practices.

Vote fraud was compounded by the introduction of a new com-

puter system designed to tabulate the votes on election night. Typically it took several days to count the results from Mexico's 54,000
polling stations, but the computerized system developed for 1988
promised instant results. As the returns started coming in on election night, officials at the interior ministry began to fear that the
election would be lost to Cárdenas. Results showed that Salinas
was losing all over the country, and by a two-to-one margin in the
Federal District. As they contemplated the problem, election officials
discovered that opposition poll watchers had hacked into the PRI
computer and could see the results. Panicked, they crashed the
election computer, and announced that a glitch in the system would
delay the tabulation of the election results for several days – until,
that is, they could be fixed to favor Salinas.

The elections commission waited until July 13 to release the official results, which had Salinas winning the election with 50.4 percent
of the vote. It was a victory, but by a considerably smaller margin
than that of any previous PRI president (de la Madrid claimed 74.3
percent). Official results also gave the PRI majorities in both houses
of Congress, but reduced their majority to 260 in the 500-seat Chamber of Deputies. This meant that the PRI now lacked the necessary
two-thirds majority for passing constitutional amendments.

Cárdenas, who was awarded 31.1 percent of the vote, immediately
challenged the election. On July 16, 200,000 people protested in the
Zócalo. Following this, Cárdenas went on a national protest tour. His
efforts were to no avail. In August the Chamber of Deputies certified
the election. Some Cárdenas supporters wanted to try to overthrow
the government, but in the end Cárdenas opted for peaceful opposition, promising to build a new political party that could challenge
the PRI in future elections. On December 1, 1988, the forty-year-old
Salinas was inaugurated president of the Mexican Republic.

The PRI's success in managing the 1988 election could not obscure
the fact that the country Carlos Salinas would rule was not the same
as it had been before the crisis. The old economy was dead and
buried. Civil society, stifled for decades by the PRI's patron–client
system, was every day growing stronger and more diverse. The political system too was in the midst of major upheavals; the PRI's

victory did little to stifle a burgeoning political opposition at the local and national levels. More than this, however, in the midst of these changes Mexicans were building links to the world beyond the nation's borders in ways that had not been seen since the creation of the revolutionary nationalist state in the 1920s. Mexico's economy, civil society, and political system were all destined to be remade as Mexico emerged as a participant in the global age. For some, this process would include dreams of Mexico finally joining the First World. For others the experience would be closer to a nightmare.

2 | Salinastroika

Carlos Salinas de Gotari, it seems, dreamed of being appointed director general of the World Trade Organization (WTO). This may seem like an insignificant piece of trivia, but it is one of those minor facts that help explain the story of the PRI between 1988 and 1994. Salinas was a man whose ambitions were global, who imagined that after he transformed Mexico into a member of the community of modern nations he would take the world stage as the leader of the organization that would define the shape of global trade in the twenty-first century. His scholarly credentials, his role in a decade of economic transformations in Mexico, and the work he undertook as president of Mexico to create the North American Free Trade Agreement (NAFTA) and democratize the political system gave him credentials that rivaled those of any other politician of his day, and prompted more than a few of his supporters to dub his presidency "salinastroika." According to his own press, he was honest, hard working, idealistic, and a selfless servant of the nation. He would hold on to this image of himself for far too long. As he angrily left Mexico City in the midst of a scandal in early 1995, and began a hunger strike in a poor neighborhood in Monterrey, he still insisted that he was a candidate for the WTO job.

This seemingly odd juxtaposition of political disgrace and his persistent hope that he might become the director general of the WTO reminds us of the dual nature of the Salinas *sexenio*,[1] which was characterized both by idealistic political and economic reforms and some of the most spectacular corruption and political violence that Mexico has ever seen. Salinas would continually try to deflect criticisms of wrongdoing, accusing those close to him, particularly his brother Raúl, of abusing his trust. He dealt similarly with questions about his own commitment to democratization (after all, had he not come to power in a fraudulent election?), repressing dissent even as he championed political openings. It is true that these strategies seem perhaps a little cynical, but we should nonetheless avoid the temptation to simply dismiss Salinas's idealism as a cover for graft or authoritarianism. Inexplicable enrichment (as it is called in the legal code) has long been a part of Mexican political life, and Salinas could reasonably have believed that an effort to enrich himself and his friends was not incompatible with a desire to act as the nation's savior. Similarly, and not unlike the Russian originator of the process from which salinastroika drew its name, Salinas was not averse to forcing his own views on recalcitrant Mexicans if he believed he knew what the country needed, even if this involved defying the PRI and the popular will.

Revenge of the technocrats

Carlos Salinas was not a beloved figure in the PRI. He was not one of those old-style caudillo politicians who seemed to promise, through the sheer power of his physical presence, to rein in an unruly nation. In fact, within the PRI he was derided as a *técnico* (technocrat) one of a group of experts with relatively little experience of politics, but with a great deal of expertise in the arcane world of macroeconomic policy. His boss, Miguel de la Madrid, was arguably the first technocrat president, but with his diminutive stature, receding hairline, and oft-caricatured ears, Salinas wore the label perfectly.

Salinas came from a prominent political family. His father Raúl was Secretary of Industry and Commerce in the Adolfo López Mateos administration (1959–64), and had once dreamed of being president himself. As a young man Carlos avoided politics, opting to earn a degree from the UNAM in 1969, and a PhD in Political Economy and Government from Harvard in 1978. He joined the PRI in 1969, and soon began training *priistas* who were destined for public office. Over time he held a number of positions within the Ministry of Finance, and in 1979 assumed a senior position in the Ministry of Planning and Budget. He was thus involved in the earliest economic openings in Mexico, the negotiations to enter the General Agreement on Tariffs and Trade (GATT), which were concluded in 1979. The GATT was extremely unpopular in the PRI, so the decision to join was delayed until 1980, and the concomitant tariff reforms put off until 1986.

Salinas played an integral part in the de la Madrid presidential campaign in 1982 (he had been a student of de la Madrid's at the UNAM), and was named chief of the Ministry of Planning and Budget in the new administration. Salinas was the budget-cutter in the de la Madrid government, and the principal agent of economic reform. He oversaw a series of reforms that were deeply unpopular in the PRI rank and file and among many business owners, but which he believed were critical to rescuing the economy. In 1984 Salinas and the technocrats convinced the administration to lift restrictions on Foreign Direct Investment (FDI). In 1986 they implemented the tariff reductions required under the GATT, lowering the maximum allowable tariff from 100 to 50 percent. Tariffs were again lowered to 20 percent in 1987, and import licenses on 91 percent of goods were eliminated.[2] Salinas was also involved in decisions to end government support for several industries. Through the combined efforts of the de la Madrid and Salinas administrations, the number of public sector firms was reduced from 1,155 to 232.

In the short run these moves further devastated the economy, but the technocrats believed that these were essential reforms to assure future economic stability. They believed that Mexico's crippling debt and economic crisis could be ameliorated only through an economic program that produced economic growth. Inasmuch as Mexico lacked the capital to produce that growth, the government needed foreign investment, and foreign investment would materialize only if the US Treasury, the IMF and the World Bank deemed Mexico creditworthy. This in turn would happen only if the Mexican government embraced free market economics and reduced the size of the public sector. The technocrats could have implemented a moratorium on payments or demanded debt forgiveness, but rejected these confrontational approaches because they believed that they would lead to further disaster. Instead, they agreed to most of the terms demanded by the IMF, and asked for a rescheduling and slight reduction of the debt in return.

Their efforts paid off in 1987 when Mexico signed a debt rescheduling plan proposed by US Secretary of the Treasury James

A. Baker III. The Baker Plan allowed for a twenty-year repayment schedule for debt contracted prior to 1985. Eighty-three percent of the $52.2 billion public debt and $9.7 billion of private debt that Mexico had contracted before 1985 would be repaid in this period, with a seven-year grace period. At the same time, multilateral lending agencies and banks promised the government another $12.5 billion in loans to help the Mexican economy grow.

Efforts to reduce inflation bore fruit in late 1987, in part aided by an agreement between the state, the major unions, peasant groups, and business known as the Economic Solidarity Pact. Labor groups promised to reduce their wage demands and business groups agreed to curb price increases, while the government promised to cut public spending and credit, and follow a tighter monetary policy. The value added tax (VAT) was increased, tax exemptions were eliminated, and the government increased the fees for goods and services. Interest rates were also allowed to rise in order to promote savings and reduce capital flight. Owing largely to these efforts the rate of inflation fell from 159 percent in 1987 to 52 percent in 1988.

The technocrats marveled at these numbers, but workers did not seem particularly impressed. Labor bore an inordinate share of the burden of Salinas's economic reforms, stoking anger that had been building since the early 1980s, when the de la Madrid regime implemented a program of "unilateral flexibilization" in the workplace in order to promote manufacturing for export at the expense of domestic consumption. Though at first the reforms led to large-scale strikes, CTM leaders began stifling dissent in their unions when it became clear that their personal survival was at stake. When the CTM signed the pact in 1987, more than a few union members openly complained that workers' wages were fixed at rates lower than inflation.

The nadir in Salinas's relations with organized labor may have come during the 1988 election campaign, when Joaquín Hernández Galicia (known as La Quina), the leader of the PEMEX workers' union, paid for a pamphlet that made public an incident from 1951, in which Salinas and his brother Raúl killed a family servant. The tragedy occurred after the brothers discovered a loaded rifle in their father's closet, and decided to play a game of execution. They chose a twelve-year-old maid as the victim. In a testament to the power of the Mexican oligarchy, the only punishment the brothers received was mandatory counseling.

One would not expect Salinas to forget his humiliation at the hands of La Quina, and it did not take long for him to exact his revenge. After publicly declaring that his administration was going to rein in union corruption, on the morning of January 10, 1989 federal agents broke down La Quina's doors and carted him off to jail. As the leader of a notoriously corrupt union, La Quina made an easy target. For years the union had acted as almost a state within the state. It had the right to bid without competition for "social contracts," which were worth 2 percent of the value of PEMEX's production. It ran its own social services programs and stores, and enriched the leaders of the 200,000-member union by giving them the power to sell jobs and run an elaborate patronage system. La Quina was the absolute ruler, a fact underlined by the frequent deaths of his opponents in the union.

La Quina was not a popular figure in Mexico, where the public was increasingly critical of the oil monopoly. Mexicans from across the spectrum lamented the fact that PEMEX lacked the resources to modernize production, had a bloated payroll, and an atrocious public safety record, but reform was impossible because of the power of the workers' union. This perhaps explains why public support for Salinas swelled after La Quina's arrest, and international markets responded enthusiastically. The few wildcat strikes that followed quickly petered out, as it became clear that the public at large would not support the PEMEX unions.

Salinas hailed La Quina's arrest as a sign that Mexico was embracing the rule of law, and immediately moved against the heads of the Veracruz Dockworkers and the Journeymen and Industrial Workers Union. It did not seem to matter that the principal charges laid against La Quina were phony. It was later revealed that government interrogators forced la Quina to confess to owning of a huge cache of weapons that the military planted in his house. Hernández was also convicted of murdering a federal agent during the police raid on his house in Ciudad Madero. He was given a thirty-five-year prison sentence. It later turned out that the man had been killed in an accident in Tampico a day before the assault.

In a deeply symbolic gesture, even as the legal proceedings against La Quina were ongoing, Salinas again turned to Washington for help in restructuring the economy. La Quina's imprisonment was offered as a sign that the days of old-style unionism, protectionism, and clientelism were over, and that the new Mexico would play by the rules of the international marketplace. In March 1989 Salinas reached a deal with US lenders to restructure Mexico's $57.2 billion long-term commercial debt. In July 1989 Mexico signed an agreement with 500 international creditors to the same effect. Together these deals reduced Mexico's foreign debt by 6 percent. Mexico's international fortunes improved even further in 1990, when Salinas embraced a plan proposed by Nicolas Brady, secretary of the US Treasury. The Brady Plan promised debt relief in return for fiscal reform and guarantees that debts could be collected. In order to comply with the Brady Plan Mexico would need to reduce government spending, practice fiscal discipline, and open the economy to foreign trade and investment. The deals also required that Mexico's debt become a commodity that could be traded in international markets, a reform that would force an unprecedented level of transparency into government dealings.

Openings

Salinas and the technocrats believed they had reason to be optimistic about the prospects for these reforms. Mexico was a low-wage country, with easy access to the largest consumer market in the world. The country already exported a variety of agricultural and mineral products to the US, and under the auspices of the Border Industrialization Program (popularly known as the Maquila Program, begun in 1965[3]) assembly plants in northern Mexico were sending a steadily growing stream of manufactured goods to the north. Yet the national economy Salinas inherited was weighed down with the negative legacies of a history of protectionism. Monopolies, abuse, and indiscriminate subsidies still protected a small number of producers at the expense of a majority of the population.

A first obvious step in economic reform lay in opening the entire Mexican economy to the trade and investment that had characterized the Maquila Program for two decades. This seemed particularly urgent to the technocrats. Given Mexico's high debt and low rate of domestic savings, foreign investment in the Mexican economy was crucial to economic recovery. Salinas tried to improve Mexico's trade and investment climate by pursuing trade agreements with a host of partners. He signed bilateral trade agreements with the Central American Community, Chile, Colombia, Bolivia, and Venezuela, and negotiated Mexico's entry into Asia-Pacific Economic Cooperation (APEC). Still, since the United States accounted for 73 percent of Mexico's foreign trade, Salinas believed that efforts to expand trade and investment needed to focus on the US as well.

American politicians were skeptical about the prospects of a trade deal with Mexico, given the threat to American workers, but business and industrial interests in Canada (having just signed a free trade agreement with the US, Canada had to be included), the US, and Mexico responded positively to the idea of a trade agreement when Salinas first proposed it. North American producers were attracted to Mexico by low wages, lax environmental regulation, and easy access to North American markets, which taken together offered the possibility of increasing profitability dramatically. Many North American manufacturers were already in life-or-death struggles to increase profitability and cut prices (the first to compete on the stock market, and the second to compete in the marketplace), and Mexico could help in both these endeavors. In the end, it was the promise of economic growth, a general belief in free trade in the mainstream of both political parties, and aggressive lobbying on the part of business interests which made the trade agreement with Mexico appealing in the US. Similar forces were at work in Canada, where the major parties supported the agreement, and the leftist New Democratic Party had reached its lowest levels of support in a generation.

Secret negotiations between the three governments were concluded in December 1992, with the agreement that North American Free Trade Agreement (NAFTA) would come into force on January 1, 1994. NAFTA created a block of 400 million consumers and represented a third of the world's GDP ($8 trillion in 1994). The treaty immediately opened US and Canadian markets to 84 percent of Mexican exports, with the remaining barriers removed in increments of five to fifteen years.

A difficult transition to modernity [4]

Salinas believed trade and investment opportunities were important, but beyond this he knew that Mexico had to make its own "difficult transition to modernity." During decades of inward-oriented development, Mexican public finances had been impossibly opaque; budgets were manipulated indiscriminately by presidents who used the federal government like a personal slush fund. This arrangement was unacceptable to the technocrats, who believed that the abuse of public finances was ultimately detrimental to Mexicans as a whole. Salinas began to rectify this situation when he granted the Central Bank functional and administrative autonomy along lines that made it similar to its northern cousin. He also reformed the tax code, lowering personal taxes and the VAT, and gave workers who earned the minimum wage subsidies to increase their income. In part owing to his reforms of the tax system he was able to reduce tax evasion, which was endemic in Mexico. He managed to expand the number of taxpayers by 45 percent, increasing taxes collected by the federal government by 32 percent (in real terms) by 1994. Salinas also tried to balance the budget, reducing public expenditures by 25 percent in real terms during his *sexenio*.

Much of the reduction in government spending came from two sources: price increases for a number of commodities (including diesel, natural gas, and electricity) and divestment of state-owned companies (parastatals). During the Salinas administration 415 parastatal companies were privatized, amounting to 67 percent of those controlled by the government in 1988. Prominent among these were TELMEX, the aviation companies, the chemical sector, insurance, hotels, radio stations, and the banks (the number of banks was reduced from 764 to eighteen). In some cases privatizations provided the government with a windfall profit. The banks, for example, were sold for three times their book value. On the other hand, many of the privatizations simply eliminated poorly performing companies that had been nationalized in the first place only because they were facing bankruptcy. Traditionally it has been a standard practice of the government to save failing companies and the jobs they provided through nationalization. It also provided businessmen with an extremely important social safety net, reducing the risks associated with business failures. Lately, however, it had placed an enormous weight on public finances.

Salinas believed that these privatizations would prompt a surge in investment and help create a modern national infrastructure. Other projects, including efforts to promote private road building and limited privatization in the electrical sector, were justified with the same logic. This meant that a series of public goods would no longer be provided by the state, but Salinas promised that the private sector would provide these goods more efficiently and effectively than the Mexican state, helping Mexico compete in the international marketplace.

Privatizations were a controversial undertaking in Mexico, in part because of perceptions that the process was corrupt. Salinas's friend Carlos Peralta Quintero won a concession to build a cellular telephone network. He then sold 42 percent of the network to Bell Atlantic for $1.04 billion in 1993. Around the same time he gave $50 million to Raúl Salinas, the president's brother, for reasons that have never been satisfactorily explained. Controversy also dogged the bank privatizations, as some of the banks were granted to individuals with questionable credentials. Some of the new owners used their banks to launder drug money, or made illegal loans to themselves and their friends, causing several banks to fail. In at least one case the new owners made huge cash contributions to the PRI, raising the specter of illegal pay-offs for favors in the privatization process.

Controversy also surrounded the privatization of Telmex, the telephone monopoly. A group of employees proposed that the company be sold to its workers, but Salinas instead decided to offer the company to Carlos Slim Helú (his campaign manager) and a group of investors. Slim purchased the company in 1990 for $1.76 billion, with the stipulation that the privatized Telmex receive a six-year monopoly on the Mexican telephone service. Owing largely to the low price and protections offered to the company by the government, his investment quintupled in value in just two years. Telmex stock increased Slim's personal wealth to $4.4 billion by the end of the Salinas presidency.

Telephone service did improve, but privatization was a mixed blessing for consumers. Protected from competition, Telmex

increased its fees for local service by 40 percent, maintained pro-
hibitively expensive installation charges (around $300), and did
little to reduce the incredibly long waiting period for obtaining
service (averaging six months). Billing irregularities and poor service continued to be a problem in many areas, prompting 114,000
complaints about Telmex to the government in 1993 alone.

Salinas may also have wanted to privatize PEMEX, but the risks
were simply too high. Not only did he rely on PEMEX and its unions
as a critical source of PRI support (financial and otherwise), but he
risked a political disaster if he sold this symbol of revolutionary
reform (President Lázaro Cárdenas nationalized oil in the midst of a
conflict with foreign oil companies in 1938). PEMEX, along with the
Federal Electrical Commission (CFE), was an inefficient albatross,
rife with corruption and crippled by antiquated infrastructure, but
Salinas dared not attack it directly. Instead, he made flanking attacks
on both companies. He reclassified the oil industry into two sectors
(basic and secondary), and allowed limited foreign investment in the
secondary sector. He also authorized foreign companies to generate
electricity for their own use. If they had excess power, it could then
be sold to the CFE.

Privatizing the social contract

Salinas wanted to extend market economics into three areas that
most Mexicans felt were undeniable "public goods," education, social services, and pensions. Among the great accomplishments of the
revolution, these systems provided a social safety net for millions of
workers. Yet a decade of crisis ravaged these public trusts. Schools
lacked teachers, supplies, and even basic repairs. The four hundred
thousand students at the UNAM often toiled without professors,
laboratory equipment, or functioning programs. Lagging government subsidies and high levels of unemployment (which limited
worker contributions) devastated the Institute for State Workers
(ISSSTE) and the Mexican Social Security Institute (IMSS).[5] It is little
wonder that by the late 1980s the IMSS was often known by an
alternative interpretation of the Spanish acronym: "nobody cares
about your health."

Some contemporary economists argue that each of these programs could have returned to past effectiveness if provided with even modest budget increases, but this was not on the Salinas agenda. Claiming resource limitations, but informed by an ideological commitment to the market, Salinas maintained that privatization was the only way to revive each of these public trusts. He reformed Article 3 of the constitution to allow private educational entities the same access to state subsidies as public schools. Salinas also pressed the public universities to charge tuition as a means of raising money and improving facilities. The move was extremely unpopular among the poor (most of whom would never go to a university but wanted the option to be available to their children) and among students in the public schools, but was met by many in the middle classes with indifference or even support. Since there was little chance that the state would expand funding to the levels needed to repair the UNAM's reputation, for the middle class and elites (precisely the groups that had abandoned these institutions) this seemed like the only means of restoring some credibility to the system.

Catholic schools, the *bête noire* of the revolutionary state, also benefited from these reforms. Salinas allowed the Church to teach religion in private schools for the first time since the 1910s. The Church was also given the right to own property, and priests were given the right to vote and wear clerical dress in public, all direct departures from past practices. Religious icons – crucifixes, statues of the Virgin of Guadalupe – long banned from public schools and the subject of violent confrontations in the past, found their way into schoolrooms around the country.[6]

When it came to social welfare and pensions, Salinas again advocated a market approach, based in part on a series of World Bank proposals. To provide retirement funds for workers, he introduced a private Retirement Savings System (SAR), in which 2 percent of workers' salaries were put aside for retirement and disability. By 1994 the new system was administering retirement funds for 12 million workers. Salinas's program would be followed by a 1995 Social Security Law that established private pensions.[7] The new compulsory program emphasized privatization, savings, and expansion of the financial market, and represented the largest ever transfer of public funds to private financial enterprises. Workers had the option of choosing to invest in a number of different financial entities, most of which were owned by banks or insurance companies, and which would charge fees for their services.

In health and welfare, Salinas favored an approach that placed most Mexicans into private insurance programs while offering specific programs for the very poor.[8] Those who could not afford health insurance were covered under a new "Basic Package" paid for by the government, but the healthcare benefits under this package were much reduced. Poverty programs, which in the past had been universal and oriented toward integrated community development, were remade to target specific needs. The centerpiece of these efforts, the National Solidarity Program (PRONASOL), which was financed by the proceeds of privatizations, was selective in its approach, aimed at cost efficiency, and required communities to contribute labor and resources to projects. PRONASOL oversaw investments in infrastructure, communications, streets, schools, electricity, hospitals, social services, scholarships, and aid. Salinas claimed that this program needed to bypass traditional political networks if it was to be truly effective, and administered PRONASOL directly from the President's Office. A useful by-product of this decision was that this generally popular program provided a direct link between grateful peasants and their president, offering new opportunities to build support networks for the PRI.

Agricultural reform

Land is not just a commodity in Mexico; it has been at the center of political conflicts for centuries. Mexico's rural poor have long struggled against large landowners over control of land, timber, and water resources. Rural Mexicans identify deeply with their *pedazo de tierra*, which they do not view as a simple commodity. It is instead an integral part of personal and community survival, over which generations of community members have spilt their blood. Community lands were guaranteed through Article 27 of the 1917 Constitution, which at the height of the land reform process in the 1930s provided one in three Mexicans with land. Land reforms slowed to a trickle in the 1940s, but remained one of the critical instruments of agrarian politics in Mexico even in the 1990s. When

Salinas assumed office thousands of rural communities had land claims pending at the Ministry of Agrarian Reform. As long as those claims remained unresolved, there was reason to maintain peace with the Mexican state.

It should thus be unsurprising that land reform is a sensitive political issue, and open to a great deal of manipulation and demagoguery. Nearly 30,000 *ejidos* (agricultural communities created as a result of the 1910 Revolution) took up more than 50 percent of national territory in 1988. This represented 103 million hectares of the 197 million hectares of the national land mass. These lands were held by 3.5 million *ejidatarios* (heads of family), but owned collectively by their communities, which could not sell or mortgage the land. To criticize the *ejido* was to attack the nation's most vulnerable, and to betray the Revolution itself.

Salinas was not intimidated. In the *ejido* he saw a deeply troubled institution that had long since ceased to be a source of social justice. Very little land had been granted in decades, and given the scarce land resources that remained in Mexico, it seemed unlikely that there was much more to give. *Ejidos* generally lacked irrigation, fertilizer and access to agricultural credit. They were often run by small cliques that ruled through intimidation and violence, monopolizing resources for a few while the rest of the community languished in poverty. Succeeding generations of *ejidatarios* had also been relegated to smaller and smaller plots, often too small or barren to be workable, forcing millions of them to abandon the land. Making matters worse over time millions of hectares of *ejido* land had passed out of community hands, illegally rented or colonized by adjacent landowners, who because of their wealth or private title to land could borrow money, expand their operations, and prosper.

Salinas believed that the answer to these problems, and to the problems of agriculture more generally, lay in the free market. He first eliminated or sharply reduced tariffs on most agricultural products, and reduced or eliminated subsidies and credit for agriculture, ending price guarantees for all but maize and beans. He then canceled Mexico's crop insurance program, and ordered the principal agency charged with agricultural credit, BANRURAL, to refocus its energies on those peasants who were deemed potentially profitable. BANRURAL, which had long maintained an extensive portfolio of unpaid loans in order to fulfill a political mandate, would now be required to work according to the dictates of the market.

Salinas also privatized the fertilizer and coffee monopolies (INMECAFE and FERTIMEX), took control of export production away from export growers' associations, and privatized most of the sugar refineries. Growers of a whole series of commodities, from coffee to soybeans, would now need to compete on the market without the protection of the state, and many of the inputs they had long acquired at subsidized rates would have to be bought at the market price. The shock of the transition was somewhat softened by the Program of Direct Aid to the Countryside (PROCAMPO), which provided subsidies per hectare of cultivated land in lieu of price guarantees, but PROCAMPO could not possibly meet the needs of all cultivators.[9]

Though the privatization of services would have a dramatic impact on small farmers, it was Salinas's plan to allow the privatization of *ejidos* which was most controversial. Explained as an act of "justice and liberty," Salinas's 1992 reform of Article 27 proposed that smallholders be given private title to their lands, so that they could sell, rent, and mortgage their properties. This would remove restrictions on the land, and undermine the intermediaries who had dominated peasant life since the end of the 1930s. Salinas claimed that the principal losers would not be the rural poor, but the political bosses.

The reform linked privatization and productivity to future increases in the rural standard of living. It allowed peasants to buy, sell, or rent lands without permission from the *ejido*, enter partnerships to invest in land, and allowed the *ejido* itself to be dissolved with a two-thirds vote of the *ejidatarios*. Outsiders would be allowed to invest in and rent *ejidos*, and private commercial enterprises would be permitted to purchase *ejido* lands. Land could be used as collateral, though it could not be lost; the lender could only obtain the usufruct only in cases of default. In a similar vein, the new law restricted individual landholding on former *ejido* lands to "small property," but permitted groups of individuals or joint stock companies to hold former *ejidos*, promoting the economies of scale required for productivity and competitiveness.

Political openings

Salinas was an ardent advocate of economic reform. He was a much less fervent advocate of changes in the political system. In retrospect, it seems clear that as he undermined vested interests in the economy, he would inevitably undermine the political base of the PRI, but early in his presidency he seemed content to rule with the same authoritarian tendencies that had long animated PRI rule. In fact, he relied on the power of the Mexican presidency to implement a series of politically unpopular policies.

Mexican presidents had never faced much scrutiny for electoral fraud, and his early behavior suggests that Salinas was unprepared for public criticism.[10] In PRI strongholds in central and southern Mexico, Salinas micro-managed state and local-level politics, imposing his own lieutenants when necessary without the slightest public grumblings, in part because loyalty to the president trumped all other interests. In the north he found something entirely different. The PAN, still mobilized over the 1986 gubernatorial elections in Chihuahua, was so well organized that any suspect moves made by the PRI could bring tens of thousands of protesters to the streets. This was potentially embarrassing for a president seeking foreign investment and new trade agreements, especially because the region where the PAN was strongest was also the region most closely connected to the United States.

One of a growing number of PAN supporters was Vicente Fox Quesada, a Guanajuato businessman who turned to politics after the 1982 nationalizations. A graduate of the Universidad Iberoamericana, Fox worked for Coca-Cola for fifteen years, eventually heading the Latin American division of the company, before leaving in 1979 to help manage his family's shoe factories in Guanajuato. In the early eighties his family collateralized their properties and took dollar-denominated loans to build irrigation systems and packing plants for broccoli, cauliflower, and other vegetables for the US market. They survived the economic crisis because of their access to dollar income to offset their debts. Nonetheless, Fox grew angry enough over the incompetence and corruption in the PRI during the crisis that he ran for Congress as a member of the PAN in 1988. This was a dangerous decision; during the campaign health inspectors shut down his vegetable packing plant, the PRI encouraged local peasants to invade his land, and his campaign was constantly harassed. Even so, he won the election, and produced a lasting impression on the Mexican electorate when, in the midst of congressional debates over the outcome of the presidential election, he openly mocked the president elect's oversized features by cutting holes in the ballots and placing them over his ears.

The PRI did not allow Fox to assume a seat in the Chamber of Deputies out of largesse; they did so because in many parts of the country by the late 1980s it was becoming increasingly risky to engage in wholesale electoral fraud. Facing a PAN that had a growing war chest and activists at the local, state, and national level, the PRI made concessions where they were weak. In the first major example of this new strategy, in July 1989 Salinas conceded victory to the PAN candidate Ruffo Appel in the gubernatorial elections in Baja California Norte. Appel was unquestionably the victor in the election, and Salinas knew that if he allowed the PRI to steal the election, he would risk protests worse than those in Chihuahua in 1986. Appel was first opposition governor to take office since the Revolution.

Few celebrated this as a sign that the PRI had embraced democracy, for good reason. Salinas showed little interest in embracing democracy except in the breach, and state-level PRI politicians throughout the country did not even support it in Appel's case. They were outraged by Salinas's decision to concede the elections in Baja California. Since the PRI still controlled most of the media, and the elections commission, and had a huge advantage in campaign finance and publicity, many *priistas* believed that Salinas was making unnecessary concessions to appease foreign interests.

Opponents to democratization were further vexed when in 1990 and 1991 Salinas cajoled the PRI into working with PAN to pass a series of electoral inititatives. They passed a new Federal Elections code, and created two institutions to oversee elections, the Federal Elections Institute (IFE), and the Federal Elections Tribunal (TFE). These three reforms placed the organization and supervision of elections in non-partisan hands, and created independent tribunals to resolve disputes and punish electoral improprieties. Other reforms made it impossible for a single party to pass constitutional reforms, and increased the number of senators from sixty-four to 128 (four per state), a reform that was guaranteed to increase the presence of opposition parties in the Senate. New rules also called for more balanced election coverage in the media (the PRI's close ties to most media magnates would test this regulation).

The reforms produced fairly clean federal elections in 1991,[11] but at the state level *priistas* were slow to get the message. They stole elections in Guanajuato and San Luis Potosí in 1991, under-estimating the level of public scrutiny they would face for their misdeeds. In San Luis Potosí a group of 330 independent election observers led by Sergio Aguayo exposed the fraud in a report that was published in *La Jornada*. Though the PRI candidate, Fausto Zapata Loredo, probably won the election, Salinas was so embarrassed by the scandal that he forced him to resign. In Guanajuato, Vicente Fox organized state-wide protests after he was denied the governorship in the elections, and after a series of attacks by Mexican intellectuals in the US press, Salinas forced the PRI governor to resign. He did not name Fox – whom he loathed – as the new governor, but negotiated with the PAN to find a compromise. Fox was elected governor in the following cycle.

In the following year, with the ongoing negotiations over NAFTA as the backdrop, PAN candidates swept Chihuahua. Francisco Barrio Terrazas, denied the Chihuahua governorship in 1986, was elected governor, and a PAN candidate won the mayoralty of Ciudad Juárez. At the local level, by the end of 1992 PAN mayors ran sixty of the largest 160 municipalities in the country. This represented a major development for the entire Mexican political system, placing critical political tools into the hands of the PAN in much of the north.

The Party of the Democratic Revolution (PRD), created by Cuauthémoc Cárdenas out of the coalition that supported his 1988 campaign for the presidency, was not so fortunate. Salinas may have believed that the PRI had more to fear from the PRD than the PAN, or he may just have had a visceral hatred of the "Party of the Aztec Sun," because when it came to negotiations with Cuauthémoc Cárdenas's new center-left party he was much less compromising. The PRD was strongest through central and southern Mexico, traditional PRI heartlands, and local officials showed no mercy in attacking PRD candidates. In early 1990 fraudulent elections in Guerrero resulted in riots in Acapulco and Ixtapa, but local and national *priistas* gave no quarter. In November, elections in Mexico State yielded the same results, with renewed rioting, and the PRI used widespread violence to ensure its success. In both cases, Salinas remained silent. Over the six years of his presidency 250 PRD activists were killed in conflicts with the PRI. It was only after Americas Watch released a report condemning the regime for these murders in June 1990 that Salinas took any action, creating a National Human Rights Commission. The commission heard complaints in eighty-two cases in which members of the PRD were killed during the Salinas presidency, but proved almost completely ineffective in exposing the crimes and bringing the perpetrators to justice.

Critics on the left were quick to point out that the PRD was singled out for repression because at the end of the day the PRI and the PAN had very similar stances on the economy and foreign trade. Both parties were committed to a path that would integrate Mexico into the global economy and eliminate most of the vestiges of the populist state. The PRD did not represent the polar opposite of this view, as many in the party hierarchy supported freer trade, but it was the only party overtly committed to defending the rights and interests of Mexico's poor. Moreover, unlike the PAN, which drew much of its support from people who had never identified with the PRI, the PRD fancied itself as a democratized version of the old *priista* left. This was a somewhat rose-colored view of its democratic self, as the PRD did not act particularly democratically internally, and many party members did not have particularly strong democratic credentials. It was also a slightly fanciful view of its leftist self, except inasmuch as the party took on the nationalist, populist rhetoric that the PRI had abandoned.

This alone could explain Salinas's antipathy for the PRD, though his problems with Cárdenas were compounded by the fact that his economic policies and political strategies deeply divided his own party. Old-style *priistas* – known as the dinosaurs – had little use for Salinas's political and economic reforms, and in fact believed that the key to Mexico's political stability (and naturally their own power) lay in the populist state that the PRI had created over several decades. Salinas was destroying that state, and along with it the basis for the PRI as the national party. In their minds, he was also destroying the country.

Winners, losers, and also-rans

Five years into his presidential term, it was hard to find too many public critics of Carlos Salinas. Commercial and foreign interests were so delighted with him that there was even talk in some circles of amending the constitution to allow him to run for a second term. His record across the economy suggested that salinastroika had produced a remarkable series of successes. The GDP, which had declined 8 percent from 1981 to 1987, grew by 23 percent between 1988 and 1994.[12] GDP growth exceeded population growth in most of these years. Much of the growth came through exports, especially in the *maquila* sector. In 1982 Mexican exports totaled $24 billion. By 1994 they exceeded $60 billion. These numbers would only improve under NAFTA, as exports from Mexico to the US surged by 22 percent in 1994. In that same year manufactured exports in 1994 increased by 27 percent.

Salinas's growth-oriented program had a dramatic impact on the fundamentals of the Mexican economy. A public sector deficit that was 5.2 percent of GDP in 1989 became a surplus of 2 percent in 1992 and 3.4 percent 1993. Inflation, which had been at 159.2 percent in 1987, fell to 19.7 percent in 1989, rose to 29.9 percent in 1990 (owing largely to Salinas's decision to raise prices for public services to meet expenditures), but fell thereafter. Inflation was only 7.1 percent in 1994. Domestic interest rates fell from 52 percent per month in 1988 to 13.6 percent per month in 1994. After falling to 2,295 to the US dollar during the de la Madrid administration, during the Salinas presidency the peso lost only 43 percent of its value. On January 1, 1993 a new peso was introduced, which traded at approximately 3.1 to the dollar. Perhaps most critically, Mexico's external debt fell from 50 percent of GNP in 1988 to 17 percent in 1994. Internal debt also fell, from 20 percent of GNP in 1988 to 5 percent in 1994. Salinas even retired $25 billion in foreign debt.

Foreign investors were encouraged by Salinas's successes, and after a decade of flight, capital flows from abroad into the Mexican economy increased tenfold 1989–93, from $3.2 billion to $32.6 billion. These investments produced rates of return that in some cases were over 50 percent per year. Crowning these achievements, in 1994 Mexico was granted admission to the WTO and the Organization for Economic Cooperation and Development (OECD), the latter commonly known in Mexico as the "club of rich nations."

Other economic indicators were not quite so encouraging. Mexico's current account deficit grew from $6 billion in 1982 to almost $30 billion in 1994. Foreign investment accounted for much of this amount, and turned the trade balance from a surplus of 0.2 percent of GDP in 1989 to a deficit of 3.3 percent in 1993. Mexico also maintained a consistent trade imbalance in foodstuffs during the Salinas years (over $1 billion per year). Consumption and personal debt also skyrocketed from 1989 to 1993 (consumption at 4.9 percent per year), leading to a very low rate of domestic savings. These trends made it increasingly difficult to maintain the value of the peso. By 1994 critics feared that it was overvalued by 15 percent.

Foreign investment made the Bolsa (the Mexican stock market) one of the most dynamic emerging markets in the world during the early 1990s. In fact, much of the foreign investment that came into Mexico went into speculative ventures in the Bolsa instead of productive activities. For instance, in 1992 more than half of the $60 billion invested in Mexico was invested in the Bolsa, pushing prices up and making the market extremely vulnerable to the whims of investors who would exit the market at the slightest sign of trouble. Salinas introduced the *tesobono* – a government bond pegged to the US dollar – to diminish the potential for volatility in the market, only to discover later that this decision created a whole new series of potential problems for the economy.

Employment conditions did improve during the Salinas *sexenio*. The number of people employed with benefits from IMSS increased by 26 percent between 1988 and 1994, and unemployment levels fell in all years but 1993. Average salaries for workers increased by 22 percent in real terms, and the Pact for Stability and Economic Growth (PECE), signed in October 1993, assured workers that increases in the minimum wage would be tied to the rate of inflation and increases in productivity. Though social spending lagged in some areas, by 1994 social expenditures surpassed 54 percent of discretionary spending, up from 32 percent in 1989. Old age pensions were also significantly increased by IMSS. Similarly, in 1993 PRONASOL spent 52 billion new pesos on 523,000 projects in poor communities. Even though social spending remained low compared to pre-crisis levels, PRONASOL's share of GDP rose from 0.3 percent in 1989 to 0.8 percent in 1994. As a result, under Salinas the number of Mexicans living in extreme poverty fell from 15 million to 13.5 million.

Increasingly confident in the Mexican market, in March 1993 PepsiCo announced that it would open Pizza Huts, KFCs, and Taco Bells in Mexico. They joined a growing number of transnational companies, including Sears, Wal-Mart, Home Depot, and others who were opening retail outlets in the country, marking the beginning of a decade in which more than a hundred transnational companies, the vast majority of them US-based, entered the Mexican market. Beyond signaling that the era of protectionism was over and indicating that market forecasters saw an increasingly prosperous Mexican middle class in the future, these retail outlets transformed the look, feel, and smell of the Mexican urban landscape. Some called it imperialism, but to the millions of consumers who rapidly made Wal-Mart the largest retailer in the country, it smelled like the First World.

Middle-class Mexicans were not so enthusiastic about the people who sat on the streets, begging in front of the McDonald's as they went inside for their Happy Meal. In the early 1990s the few pesos that one of these meals cost was little enough by North American standards, but could represent half of a worker's daily earnings. And while Salinas produced statistics that suggested that the living standards of the poor were improving, there was a great deal of evidence to demonstrate that the budget surpluses of the Salinas years were produced in part through a systematic decline in the purchasing power of the middle and working classes. The wage increases of the early 1990s were not distributed evenly, and most low-skilled wage workers and the growing proportion of workers in the informal sector saw few benefits. In some parts of the informal economy half the workers were women, and one-quarter were children. The latter generally worked in the export agriculture sector, earning extreme poverty wages.

The disparities of this process are starkly revealed by the fact that between 1987 and 1994 Mexico welcomed twenty-one new billionaires, while the minimum wage lost 40 percent of its value. Even with some workers seeing gains, by 1992 wages were still only three-quarters of what they were in 1979. The pacts Salinas signed with the unions ensured that this trend would continue. Salinas used the labor codes to hold down the minimum wage during his term in office, with the result that in many areas wages remained depressed in spite of gains in productivity.

Working and poor Mexicans thus had a deeply mixed experience under salinastroika. For those with access to jobs in the burgeoning export sector, Salinas offered the first real wage increases many had seen in a decade. For those left behind, there were some new social programs, but those programs were more limited and politicized than in the past. For all its promise of a scientific approach to targeting poverty, PRONASOL was principally targeted at areas where it could strengthen political support for the PRI through give-aways from the president, and where it could create a stable base to support neo-liberal market reforms. Traditional leaders in the CNC and unions felt this shift acutely, as their power to distribute largesse and thus their very *modus operandi* were threatened.

Rural Mexicans took advantage of PRONASOL by the millions, but were not particularly sold on the larger promises made by Salinas. Their antipathy was most clearly evident in the response of *ejidatarios* to Article 27 reform. Rather than embracing the opportunity to privatize their lands, *ejidatarios* overwhelmingly rejected the program. So strong was their opposition that Salinas was forced to backtrack from compulsory privatization and offer it only as an option that communities could pursue if they so desired. To this date, very few communities have taken him up on the offer. Their responses to the decision by the state to curtail all future reform were similarly strident, as was evident in the Chiapas rebellion in 1994.

Rural and poor Mexicans were similarly unenthusiastic about their larger prospects under NAFTA. Sensing that they were destined to be losers in globalization, in 1993 fewer than 15 percent of Mexicans expressed enthusiasm for the treaty, while about 60 percent of the population supported it partially. One-quarter of Mexicans opposed the treaty outright. Some middle- and upper-class Mexicans could hope that the treaty would offer new opportunities in the global economy. Workers in the export sector might also gain some benefits, new jobs and new opportunities with better wages than could be found in other sectors of the economy. A relatively small number of Mexican workers might also find work with a transnational service company or retailer, both of which tended to pay better wages than Mexican employers. For the rest, including the vast majority of rural Mexicans, if they wanted to take advantage of the new economy they would need to do it as undocumented laborers in the US, slipping across the frontier in out-of-the-way places even as commodities produced by Mexican workers crossed the border freely.

3 | Nineteen ninety-four

The year 1994 is one that Carlos Salinas would probably like to forget. His troubles began on New Year's Day – the day NAFTA came into effect – in a sleepy southern region that most Mexicans barely even considered part of Mexico. Although Chiapas was the most important producer of coffee and bananas in Mexico, produced half of the country's hydroelectricity, and one-quarter of Mexico's natural gas, half of the population in this state of 3.7 million was malnourished, and 60 percent earned less than the minimum wage ($1,500 a year). Most Mexicans viewed Chiapas as backward, as on the periphery of the nation, or ignored the state altogether, and were thus stunned when the Zapatista Army of National Liberation (EZLN) announced themselves to the nation on New Year's Day. Three thousand well-trained guerrillas wearing rubber boots and home-made uniforms, some of them carrying home-made wooden rifles (others carried Sten Mark IIs, AK-47s, and Uzis), seized several towns in central and eastern Chiapas, including the old colonial capital, San Cristóbal de las Casas.[1] Their serious intentions were driven home when they attacked a nearby army base, released 179 prisoners from a nearby jail, and kidnapped a former governor.

They abandoned San Cristóbal and the other towns on 2 January, but not before making their desires known. In their first "Declaration from the Jungle," the EZLN decried centuries of abuse and injustice by declaring " ... today, we say ENOUGH IS ENOUGH. We are the inheritors of the true builders of our nation. The dispossessed, we are millions and we thereby call upon our brothers and sisters to join this struggle as the only path, so that we will not die of hunger due to the insatiable ambition of a 70 year dictatorship led by a clique of traitors." Citing Article 39 of the constitution (" ... The people have, at all times, the inalienable right to alter or modify their form of government"), the Zapatistas called for no less than the overthrow of Carlos Salinas.

Trying to limit the damage, within days Salinas offered a pardon to anyone who laid down their arms. He received a summary response from the Zapatistas' masked leader, Subcomandante Marcos, who asked, "What are you going to pardon us for?" This was fairly embarrassing for the president, who had known about an impending rebellion in the region for months, but had tried to keep the problem as quiet as possible, so as not to derail NAFTA. Since this strategy had clearly failed, he decided to fire his interior minister, José Patrocinio González Garrido (who, as governor of Chiapas, had been accused of numerous abuses against peasants), and moved 14,000 troops into the region to quell the revolt. By the time he declared a unilateral ceasefire on January 12, the dead included thirteen soldiers, seventy rebels, and 300 non-comabants. The EZLN was routed, and 60,000 people were displaced. When peace talks with the rebels began six weeks later, there were nearly 40,000 federal troops in the state.

The rebellion in Chiapas did not bode well for the Mexico Carlos Salinas imagined, and more bad news was on the way. In March the country was shaken by the assassination of Salinas's hand-picked successor, Luis Donaldo Colosio. In September, after fairly orderly elections, the secretary-general of the PRI, José Francisco Ruiz Massieu, was assassinated, leading to a botched criminal investigation and conspiracy theories that verged on the bizarre. In December the country suffered an economic meltdown that reminded Mexicans that whatever Carlos Salinas's pretensions, the First World remained a distant dream.

The first rebellion of the cyber-age

From the very beginning it was clear that the Zapatistas had ambitions that went well beyond Chiapas. They brought printed copies of the First Declaration from the Jungle with them on January 1, and the first news of the rebellion was passed to CNN in a phone call from Chiapas on that same day. Telecommunications allowed the rapid dissemination of their declaration to a global audience, generating a profile for the movement before the Mexican government could put its own spin on events (the government wanted to suggest that the rebellion was the work of foreigners). In the past, when Mexico lacked an effective opposition press and dissidents lacked access to the means to tell their stories, government efforts to dismiss the EZLN might have worked, but in 1994 magazines, newspapers, the electronic media, and a growing number of independent organizations had an unprecedented ability to get the story out. Journalists flooded into the region to "meet the Zapatistas" even as troops were moving in, and their reports exposed every federal move and further fueled public support for the Zapatistas. A relatively insignificant military skirmish thus quickly turned into a very effective propaganda war.

The Mexican public was captivated. Zapatista attacks on both Salinas and NAFTA provided a powerful expression of the suffering that millions of Mexicans had faced during the Salinas *sexenio*, and within days the myth of shared prosperity under Salinas seemed to unravel. Expressions of popular support for the EZLN started to pop up around the country. One hundred thousand demonstrated in support in Mexico City's Zócalo on January 12, the day Salinas declared the ceasefire. The bandanas and ski masks that signified "Zapatista" became ubiquitous in public spaces, and dolls made up as Zapatistas appeared in markets around the country. In short order Zapatistas became characters in cartoons and the nation grew obsessed with uncovering the secret identity of the enigmatic Marcos. It is little wonder that the Zapatistas rapidly assumed rock-star status on the left. Marcos T-shirts even briefly threatened to overtake the image of Che Guevara as an icon of social protest.

As the public demanded more information from and about the EZLN, and the traditional media proved reluctant to satisfy that demand, the war shifted to the Internet. Annoyed that they could find only edited copies of Zapatista communiqués, in early 1994 Zapatista sympathizers began e-mailing the entire contents of all Zapatista communications. A virtual community was born, dedicated to disseminating information and building support across continents. For his part, Marcos proved brilliant at fueling the growth of the support network. His language was wistful, poetic, playful, sometimes humorous, and filled with rhetorical flourishes that captivated many on the international left. To be sure, he was strident, but his rhetoric was nothing like the wooden, Stalinist language of an earlier generation of revolutionaries.

Supporters of the Zapatistas could also participate vicariously in the rebellion by getting their information on the EZLN in spite of efforts by the Mexican government to spin the story another way. They were, in effect, a part of the rebellion against globalization through the very act of logging on to the Internet and getting the story from the source. As they traveled through cyber-space to the Lacandón forest, they could imagine that, in spite of knowing very little about Mexico or Chiapas, they were seeing things as they really were, reassured by the sense of authenticity created by reading *actual* declarations from the jungle, seeing the *actual* faces (even if they were covered by masks) of their newest heroes. At its worst, this allowed activists to use the EZLN as a metonym for their own opposition to NAFTA, dislocating the rebellion almost entirely from its historical and regional roots.

The relative novelty of the Internet intensified this sensibility. Major commercial ventures had yet to find effective ways to saturate this new medium, and early theorists of the World Wide Web advocated it as a profoundly democratic phenomenon, an opportunity, as it were, for every individual to act as their own printing press, bypassing the traditional media and the multinationals that seemed to control the flow of information across the planet. Zapatistas were rooted in place by their indigenousness, their claims to be stewards of the land, and their claim to specific pieces of land, yet they were cyber-savvy in a way that suggested something entirely new, something that bypassed the nation and connected them to a global community of dissidents. For their part, supporters could fairly believe that as long as the Zapatistas remained connected to a vibrant community on the Internet, the Mexican government would be reluctant to silence them through violent means.

If direct access to the Zapatistas through the Internet provided a sense of immediacy, their rhetorical decision to link their demands to a 500-year struggle for indigenous self-determination provided many supporters outside of Mexico with another critical reason to support the EZLN; they combined the romantic revolutionary and the authentic *indigene* in an intoxicating blend. Rigoberta Menchú had just won the Nobel Prize. The International Labor Organization had declared itself in favor of indigenous self-determination. Using terms like "from time immemorial" and "ancestral lands," Zapatistas directly accessed the sympathies of a network of international readers and activists.

Zapatismo has tended to produce simple and powerful imagery that evokes the great social justice claims of our day. Humanitarian groups were moved by the images of poverty from the region. Feminists were inspired by the "Women's Revolutionary Law," with which the EZLN supposedly took aim at patriarchy. Environmentalists were impressed by their harmonious relationship with nature. Human rights groups could not but be moved by the injustices they faced at the hands of the state and local elites. More than this, members of all these communities were impressed by the seemingly organic democracy practiced in Zapatista villages. Many insisted that, as per his title, Marcos was merely a sub-comandante, obeying the will of the people.

On the Web fanciful imagery predominated (and continues to do so). Consider the following: "The EZLN is, now and forever, a hope. And the hope, like the heart, is on the left side of the chest. We are now the product of all of you, of your word and of your nourishment."[2] Similarly, environmental and essentialist images collide. "Chiapas is the ancestral lands of the Maya. They shouldn't have to give up their land, their language, or their culture ... As of right now, only 12% of Mexico's Lacandón Jungle remains intact, and they (as well as the rest of the Earth) need to protect this rainforest, not to have it sold to paper companies."[3] Websites commonly represent the rebellion in Chiapas as the great clarion call against globalization, symbolized by the fact that "the cry of *Zapata Vive!* can now be heard on the internet, on the streets and in cities across the world."[4] At their most narcissistic, advocates in the north also claim that "while the rebellion in Chiapas may at first glance appear to be a million miles away from the reality of life ... the parallels are not hard to spot."[5]

As with all things that take place in cyber-space, this was a new reality, and did not need to be connected to any other. On the Net *Narco-News* and the *New York Times* look like similarly authoritative sources of information, and readers are left to believe those stories which they like the best. In the case of Chiapas it did not matter that the declarations were fanciful, and often unconnected to day-to-day life in Chiapan communities; they captivated the imagination of a growing network of solidarity groups, which used the EZLN as a free-floating signifier of their oppositional status. It is in this context that Marcos could appear as the follower, and not the powerful leader that he was, and Zapatistas could appear to have achieved greater gender equality than anywhere else in Mexico. These claims did not need to be verified. The Web also allows the Zapatista supporters to embrace the postmodern pastiche that alternately infuriates and captivates the contemporary left. Until recently, Speedy Gonzalez, with mask and pipe, welcomed viewers to the official website of the EZLN.[6]

Behind the masks

Lost in the propaganda wars, of course, were the actual Zapatistas. Very few of the 3,000 people who took up arms on January 1, 1994 will ever see a web page; most do not even have electricity in their home communities. They did not rebel with the goal of becoming darlings of the international left, nor did most have a particularly clear understanding of the intricacies of NAFTA. Rebellion is a very dangerous business, and historically most rebels have made demands that reflect a very specific set of wants and needs, rooted in local circumstances. Chiapas was no exception.

As recently as the 1950s, village life in the Chiapas highlands was relatively stable. Male villagers often migrated out to work, but government, religion, and *cargos* (communal responsibilities) functioned to maintain relative social peace within villages. Indigenous communities were stratified, but the *cargo* duties owed by wealthy and powerful village men tended to ameliorate some of the village inequality. Consent of the governed was necessary for rule (both through formal assemblies and informal relations), and the emphasis on communal cohesion tended to mute the impact of outside influences.

Life in the highlands began to change rapidly after the Mexican state established offices for the National Indigenous Institute (INI) in San Cristobal in 1951. The INI was a classic modernizing force;

it aimed to open schools and medical clinics, and modernize agriculture in indigenous communities. INI officials often supported bilingualism and local cultural practices, but were mandated by the Mexican state to modernize – and Mexicanize – the Indian.[7] The INI was never wholly successful, but in part through its efforts to reduce infant mortality a growing population soon saw improved economic opportunities and increased conflicts over land. Market and state penetration exacerbated class stratification, and the traditional systems began to falter. This breakdown was most acute in the regions where land reforms gave peasants access to land on former coffee estates (*fincas*). Former landless laborers became coffee cultivators, but the benefits tended to be limited to a small number of individuals, who ruled the region through political bosses. Many young people were unable to acquire land for cultivation and increasingly found themselves in conflict with the bosses. Some of the marginalized converted to Protestant religions and tried to challenge the system from within. Others began to migrate to the Lacandón forest, moving to towns like Las Margaritas, Ocosingo, and Altamirano, the future heartland of the EZLN.

In the late 1950s the Lacandón forest became Mexico's last frontier. Migrants came from other parts of Chiapas to escape land hunger, counting on the long-standing revolutionary promise that the state would eventually recognize their holdings. Between 1960 and 1970 the population of Las Margaritas, Ocosingo, and Altamirano grew from 30,000 to 75,000. The migrants formed colonies, requested *ejidos*, and built new communities without the traditional elders and PRI bosses. In contrast to the highlands, where boss rule became more entrenched over time, communities in the Lacandón generally functioned along democratic lines. Assemblies in the region tended to spread *cargo* responsibilities broadly, and consensus played a critical role in local decision making. Many places even lacked bosses. Their communities were also generally multilingual, with significant numbers of Protestants, some of whom had been expelled from highland communities. As might be expected, the ethnic affinities of Ch'ols, Tzotzils, Tzeltals, and Tojolabals began to break down.

Even though the region offered opportunities for liberation from a repressive political and social order, newcomers from the highlands found the Lacandón hot and inhospitable. They faced a very difficult time coping with poor soils, erosion, and constant conflict with loggers, ranchers, and other settlements. They expanded the pasturage in the region by 40 percent in just over twenty years, but many from the highlands planted poorly chosen crops, and worked the land too intensively. After they cut down the forests and exhausted the land, they moved on.

For its part the government was inconsistent in granting rights. Decisions to recognize some landholdings and not others exacerbated conflicts in the region. These conflicts grew more acute when President Echeverría granted 2,400 square miles in eastern Chiapas to the newly imagined "Lacandón tribe" in 1972. Thirty-seven Ch'ol and Tzeltal communities were ordered to vacate the region so that the new tribe, which consisted of about four hundred people, could take possession of their lands. Simultaneously a new forest agency was given the right to "manage" the forest, cutting its valuable mahogany and selling it on the market. Most communities successfully refused the demand that they leave, but the conflict highlighted the increasingly tenuous position that migrants faced in the region. This vulnerability was made even worse when President López Portillo declared much of the zone a biosphere in 1978, placing the lands off-limits to agriculture and settlement, and displacing numerous migrant communities.

During the 1980s the population of the Chiapas highlands grew by 50 percent, and conflicts over land intensified. Some individuals grew prosperous in the midst of these changes, taking advantage of political monopolies, new road systems, and their personal capital (land, tractors, trucks, and other goods) to build successful agricultural operations. Those who lacked access to capital grew desperate, and were left to eke out a living on increasingly inadequate plots of land, forced to work as laborers for their neighbors, or decided to migrate. Statistics from the region are telling: 40 percent of the population lacked any schooling, more than half of adults were illiterate, and 70 percent earned less than the minimum wage.

In part owing to population pressures in the highlands, during these years the population of the Lacandón region grew to 200,000.

Scarce lands and a growing number of petitions meant that communities in the region found themselves waiting an average of six years to see their requests for *ejidos* adjudicated. While they waited, many communities were subject to violence from ranchers, local officials, and other communities competing for the same land. When the government did offer aid to the region, the money (and land grants) went to communities that supported the PRI, while opponents of the party found themselves under attack as never before. Lacking the means to secure peace through traditional mechanisms, violence was growing more critical to PRI rule by the mid-1980s. Matters only grew worse after the international price for coffee fell by 60 percent in 1989. Thousands of small farmers in the Lacandón forest who had invested heavily in coffee faced bankruptcy.

It was thus unsurprising that in November 1991 peasants in the region responded to the proposed Article 27 reform with anger. They realized that, in spite of the reform's anti-poverty provisions, this meant that thousands of petitions for *ejidos* that were then pending would be denied. It also meant that in the future they could not hope to use agrarian reform to satiate their growing need for land. Nationally in 1991 3.5 million petitions for land remained unresolved, and 7.6 million hectares were under litigation.

Chiapans were also angered when, during the NAFTA negotiations, the Mexican state promised to end protection and price supports for maize in fifteen years. Iowa corn was less than half the price of Mexican corn, and there were 500,000 farmers in Chiapas, most of whom grew maize. Between domestic reforms and the trade treaty, Chiapans were being squeezed from all sides.

Anger spilled over into violence during an October 12, 1992 demonstration in San Cristóbal, when marchers knocked over the statue of the Spanish founder of the city. After years of disappointments and growing rage, the anti-quincentennial protests revealed an increasingly mobilized opposition, organized by a series of competing movements. Protestant churches, catechist groups, Maoist organizations, and peasant unions all found support in the desperate countryside. Their agendas were radically different, but many of these organizations provided mechanisms for indigenous Chiapans to press the state for relief.

Locals benefited from some of their efforts, winning coffee transport subsidies, and increased social spending from time to time. Federal officials grew increasingly worried about the possibility of widespread unrest around this time, and tried a number of measures to stave off crisis in the region. At various points in the early 1990s they extended government credit to peasant groups, regularized landholdings, supported peasant groups, and purchased private lands which were distributed to peasant communities. They also launched a series of programs aimed at respecting indigenous cultures, promoted bilingual education, and improved social services in the region.

The impact of these concessions is fairly easy to measure against a growing tide of support for the EZLN in Chiapas. Salinas made grand promises in Chiapas, committing $50 million from PRONASOL to the Lacandón as late as August 1993 (in all PRONASOL put $500 million into the state), but these funds simply exacerbated conflict in the region. Spending was doled out strictly according to party affiliation. To underline this point, several INI employees were jailed in Chiapas after giving PRONASOL money to PRI opponents. These actions only confirmed the counsel offered to Chiapans by the EZLN, which before the late 1980s had been a small and isolated group of erstwhile revolutionaries. Prepare for war, they said, as this is the only way to defend your rights. By early 1993 more and more local residents were listening, and the EZLN had perhaps 12,000 members under arms.

Support for the EZLN probably peaked in early 1993. At that time the state was undergoing a new wave of political violence directed by local PRI officials, and the memory of Article 27 reform was still fresh in people's minds, producing a combination of bitterness and desperation that stoked the fires of revolt. Yet as the year went on, and more federal aid poured into the state, support for a rebellion began to erode. Perhaps sensing the risky nature of revolt, during this time many potential converts to the armed struggle instead chose to align themselves with Catholic catechists, or accepted offers from PRONASOL. Fearing that their moment might pass (a fear that proved reasonable, as by January 1994 the number of Zapatista soldiers had fallen to 9,000), on March 25 the EZLN called for a vote on an uprising. The results were mixed, depending on political affiliation, recent successes and failures in obtaining *ejidos*, and class stratification within communities. In many places there was no consensus, and since consensus was generally critical to decision-making, most communities simply put off any decision.

In the end, about half the Lacandón communities voted in favor of war. Many of the communities that voted in favor of the conflict had broken with the tradition of finding consensus, and remained quite divided. In order to end the division opponents were simply ordered to leave the community. In a phenomenon that would be re-peated countless times during the following decade, the only choice that most dissenters had involved relocating to PRI-supporting, PRONASOL villages. Those who remained mobilized for war. Weap-ons were retrieved from their hiding places, training intensified, and Marcos hatched a plan for January 1. He managed to mobilize 3,000 soldiers that day, but the great majority of the 1,800 communities in the Lacandón forest did not go to war with him.

On indigenous self-determination

The recent history of struggle in the region, along with early declarations and proposals from the jungle, defined the EZLN as a peasant movement. Marcos used socialist rhetoric to defend the rebellion in early 1994, and when the first peace negotiations began with government representative Manuel Camacho Solis on February 21, the discussions focused on land, housing, work, social services, liberty, peace, democracy, and justice. Women's rights were included on the agenda, but were not central to the discussions. The same was true of the thirty-two-point accord they agreed to in early March.

Marcos and the EZLN leadership continued to pursue an agenda for reform at the national level through the long summer of 1994. Marcos desired major transformations in the Mexican political sys-tem, including reforms that went far beyond those that qualified as indigenous rights. In their Second Declaration of the Lacandón Jungle on June 12, the EZLN called for a National Democratic Con-vention for August 5–9, to be held at their "Aguascalientes,"[8] built in the community of Guadalupe Tepeyac. More than five thousand attended the convention, including state delegations, and representatives of peasant, worker, teacher, artist, health worker, student, gay and lesbian groups. The convention focused largely on the need for democracy in Mexico, and discussions revolved around thirteen specific concerns: housing, land, work, food, health, education, information, culture, independence, democracy, liberty, justice, and peace. Around the same time the EZLN ran a national poll on the Internet. One million Mexicans responded, and overwhelmingly called for a strong opposition front to the PRI, guarantees for public offices for women, and the transformation of the EZLN into a political party. Vocal political activists in Mexico and around the world were delighted by these developments. Perhaps this is why they failed to notice that many of the heroes of the struggle seemed less than thrilled.

The more far-reaching the agenda became, the less enthusiasm the EZLN found in the Lacandón. This became crystal clear when the EZLN's Second Aguascalientes Convention in November 1994 received little local support. It was at this moment that the national aspirations of Marcos and his inflated sense of destiny came directly into conflict with the rank-and-file EZLN in the region. The spectacular nature of the revolt and the outpouring of public sympathy in its aftermath were all rooted in Marcos's sweeping declarations, but many of these pronouncements found only tepid support within indigenous communities in Chiapas. Support for the armed struggle waned even among those who had voted for war, and Marcos needed to change the direction of the armed struggle in order to survive. It was at this very time that a peasant movement with national aspirations became an indigenous rights movement with a regional focus.

Indigenous Mexicans, including many of the original Zapatistas of the 1910 Revolution, have participated in regional and national movements since the colonial period. Sometimes these movements were peasant movements, at others they were religious movements, and at others they have defended entrenched conservative interests. On a political level, these movements have thus seemed quite disparate, but they have often shared in practice what they did not share in rhetoric. Indigenous Mexicans – that is, residents of communities defined by the state or self-defined as *indígena* – have historically endeavored to use their participation in larger national movements to defend local social, cultural, and political practices, systems of landholding, and economic interests. Within indigenous communities the village has traditionally been an immensely important social and political unit, and indigenous resistance, accommodation, and revolt have generally focused on defending that unit from outside interference. In this, the original Zapatistas and Cristeros (religious counter-revolutionaries of the 1920s) could share a desire to maintain certain kinds of local autonomy in the face of *hacendados*, ranchers, capitalists, and the state.

More than almost any other group in Mexico, indigenous Chiapans have traditionally prized independence at the village level as the most important means of community survival in a region where a rapacious ladino (non-indigenous Chiapan) elite treated (and treats) indigenous people almost like slaves. Communal autonomy provided indigenous Mexicans with the opportunity to live according to their own rhythms, to exist within cosmologies that were distinct not just from the larger Mexican society but from other indigenous communities as well. These were not static or hermetically sealed systems; they changed over time, and were continually contested and reshaped. Members of indigenous communities worked and lived outside their villages, in turn introducing elements of hybridity into their cultures. Yet this has not produced a homogenous Indian or mestizo national culture. Rather, the value systems, practices, and world-views of those Mexicans who ascribe to the identity *indígena* remain distinct, if distinctly modern, and are almost always defined through reference to a specific indigenous community.[9]

Even before the EZLN turned its attention to this issue, organizations like the Chiapas State Indigenous Peasant Council, and Indigenous Peoples Independent Front (both of which would work with the EZLN beginning in late 1994), placed indigenous self-determination at the top of their agenda. More than this, even if they balked at armed revolt, indigenous communities throughout the state saw the uprising as an opportunity to struggle for more freedom at the local level. Starting in February 1994, communities not affiliated with the uprising used the cover provided by the Zapatistas to drive PRI officials out of their villages and occupy adjacent lands. Shortly thereafter the Council of Indigenous and Peasant Organizations (CEOIC), which represented 280 different indigenous and peasant groups, organized a march of over a thousand protesters that descended on San Cristóbal to demand the removal of all municipal officials in the state. By the end of 1995 peasants across the state had invaded more than a thousand *fincas*, taking almost 400,000 acres of land.

Ch'ols in northern Chiapas declared a Northern Autonomous Region on October 12, 1994, indicating not just physical possession but the transformation of that space. Following their lead, in December 1994 the Zapatistas announced that they were creating thirty-eight autonomous municipalities in the region they controlled. This concept was revolutionary in Mexico. Even though in practice indigenous communities in many parts of the country have a great deal of autonomy over internal affairs, these arrangements were not legally recognized. As of December 1994 legal autonomy became the central demand of the EZLN, and would lie at the heart of all future peace negotiations.

This transformation also marked a shift in Mexican politics. After 1994 indigenous leaders would increasingly represent themselves as distinct, as "worthy in their own right" (Collier 1999). Indigenous rights had the advantage of being a sub-set of human rights, and were enshrined in a series of Mexican laws passed since the 1980s. Indigenous rights were one of the mandates of the Mexican Academy for Human Rights when it was established in 1984. In 1989 Mexico ratified the International Labor Organization's charter, which requires collective rights for ethnic and cultural minorities, and protection of indigenous communities. In 1992 Article 4 of the constitution was reformed to guarantee Indians rights within a plural nation. Collectively these developments created new institutional and legal frameworks for demanding indigenous rights, but it would take the actions of indigenous peoples themselves to ensure that these new rights were respected.[10]

That said, autonomy remains a thorny issue in the indigenous communities of Chiapas. Some indigenous communities reject autonomy outright. Other communities press for local rule in defense of their traditional practices, even as the Zapatistas sidestep those practices in order to promote their ideal of a transformed way of life in Chiapas. The EZLN continues to ignore the tradition of consensus-based decision-making, forcing their opponents to leave rebel communities. Their call for women's rights, recycling, and bans on alcohol and drugs demonstrate a desire to transform indigenous culture more than a desire to protect it.

Conflicts over the question of who possesses the rights to exploit the mineral and agricultural wealth of the Lacandón similarly remind us that the struggle for autonomy is inextricably linked to a struggle over the wealth of the region, wealth that promises to transform these communities as much as preserve them. More than this, Chiapas is already a place where the Western vision of the harmonious, closed indigenous community has long been a thing of the past (if it ever existed). This should remind us that the demand for autonomy is not so much a counter to globalization but the most effective claim that can be made within an evolving global community.

Things fall apart

The demand for indigenous autonomy is a moving target, a claim that is made within evolving political contexts, and often linked to or subsumed within a variety of other demands. Marcos himself shifted from one type of demand to another, depending on local support and international receptivity. More than this, the types of demands that indigenous peasants make depend to a large degree on the response they receive from the state. In some cases a relatively accommodating response by the state can forestall further violence, even if that response does not include an explicit outright commitment to indigenous self-determination. This seemed to be possible on March 2, 1994, when Marcos and eighteen representatives of four Mayan ethnic groups came to an agreement with government negotiators on a peace plan. The EZLN offered to lay down their arms for a series of limited concessions.[11]

The events of the following days remind us of the critical role that contingency plays in human events. Marcos and his cohort took the agreement back to the rebel territories with an air of triumph. Chief government negotiator Manuel Camacho Solis retuned to Mexico City as the most popular PRI politician in the nation, the man who had saved the country from disaster. He was so confident at that moment that he refused to deny rumors that he was pondering a run for the presidency, even though Salinas had already designated forty-four-year-old Luis Donaldo Colosio as his successor. In retrospect it seems likely that peace could have been achieved, and perhaps even possible that Camacho could have run successfully against the PRI, but for the events of March 23.

Camacho publicly disavowed any campaign for the presidency on March 22. The following day, as he campaigned in a poor Tijuana neighborhood, Colosio was shot twice from point-blank range. He was rushed to a local hospital, where he was pronounced dead several hours later. Suspicion immediately fell on Camacho, who had a history of conflict with Colosio (Colosio ousted Camacho from his position as mayor of Mexico City). When Camacho arrived for the funeral, Colosio's widow asked him to leave.

The second victim of the assassination was the peace accords. Given Camacho's role in the process, Salinas would have had a hard time selling the accords to other *priistas*, but he was spared this task when the Zapatista communities voted them down, declaring that they could not trust a government that murdered its own people. And yet Colosio's murder did more than eliminate the possibility of peace in Chiapas. Political murders were relatively common in rural Mexico, but it had been a decade since such a prominent politician had been killed. Coming shortly on the heels of another dramatic event, the murder of Cardinal Juan Jesús Posada Ocampo, the archbishop of Guadalajara, and amid a wave of well-publicized kidnappings, Colosio's assassination seemed like a sign that Mexico was on the verge of coming apart.[12]

Police quickly arrested Mario Aburto Martínez, a twenty-three-year-old who made plastic moldings in a *maquila* for about $100 per week, and accused him of Colosio's murder. He was apprehended at the scene, and after an interrogation that included beatings, he confessed that he had acted alone in shooting Colosio. Oddly, he claimed that he killed the candidate in an effort to gain media attention for his pacifist views. Aburto is now serving a forty-five-year prison sentence.

The quick arrest did little to calm Mexicans' nerves. Witnesses immediately came forward claiming a cover-up. Some claimed that Aburto was part of the security detail at the rally. Others denied that he was the man who shot Colosio, or asserted that there were multiple men who looked just like Aburto at the scene. Others alleged that the man who was presented to the public shaved, bathed, and with a new haircut, did not even look like the man arrested at the scene. A number of these allegations gained credibility when videotapes of the assassination seemed to show that the PRI security detail cleared a path for Aburto to approach Colosio so that he was just inches away from the candidate when he was shot. The gun and bullets were lost, and not a single eyewitness claimed to have seen him pulling the trigger.

The details surrounding the crime were also sketchy. Colosio was shot twice, in the head from the left, and a moment later in his stomach from the right. Many speculated that one man could not have fired both shots. Years of federal investigations and a series of botched prosecutions of alleged conspirators have yielded nothing, leaving the single-shooter theory intact. In a telling testament to the nature of public life in Mexico, to this date a majority of Mexicans remain convinced that there was a conspiracy, even though most investigations have concluded that Aburto acted alone.

Some of the rumors suggested a connection to the drug cartels, but most of the public scrutiny fell on the PRI. Camacho remained a target of rumors, though over time the most popular theory held President Salinas responsible for Colosio's death. Had Colosio angered Salinas by distancing himself rhetorically from the administration, declaring that Mexico was still part of the Third World, and needed to engage in vast political reforms in order to become a proper democracy? Some leftists within the PRI pointed to Colosio's growing popularity just before his death, and suggest that Colosio was Mexico's Robert F. Kennedy, the man who would have challenged the PRI establishment to return to its populist roots. Indeed, Colosio did launch some indirect attacks against the neo-liberal agenda of the Salinas administration, and campaigned in Mexico's impoverished communities as a social reformer who would defend the poor.

The site of his assassination, a poor shanty town where he was surrounded by 3,000 cheering supporters, only enlarges this myth. And certainly, Colosio seems to have become entangled in some serious conflicts with his mentor in the months before March – conflicts that may have left Salinas feeling betrayed by the declarations of his chosen successor. On the other hand, Salinas's defenders counter that PRI candidates commonly distance themselves from the sitting president, especially when the political winds were shifting. Efforts to court the poor would not necessarily have translated into policy changes. His close links with the architects of the neo-liberal state suggest that he would have been reluctant to scuttle most of Salinas's market reforms.

Some suspicion even fell on Salinas's choice to replace Colosio on the ticket, Ernesto Zedillo Ponce de León. Zedillo was a strong advocate of neo-liberal reform, and was the only high-level *priista* who could legally accept the nomination, having resigned his position as minister of education a year earlier in order to run the Colosio campaign. For his part, Zedillo publicly snubbed Camacho at Colosio's funeral, prompting further speculation that Camacho was behind the assassination. If, as it appeared, the PRI was at war with itself, could a nation already beset by peasant rebellion be far from collapse?

In the short run, these fears were not realized. The Bolsa did not collapse, economic chaos did not follow, and the elections went relatively smoothly. In part this was the result of an accord signed by members of the three main parties and five smaller ones in January, in which all parties renounced violence as a means for political change, and promised to create the cleanest elections Mexico had ever seen. These were the first elections in which the IFE's independence was codified in the constitution, meaning that the PRI would not have power over its governing council. Campaign spending limits were set, and the roles of election observers were expanded. New members assigned to the IFE came from across the political spectrum, from the leftist José Woldenberg to the aristocratic Santiago Creel. Members of the Civic Alliance (made up of 470 grassroots organizations), run by long-time PRI opponent Sergio Aguayo, also played a critical role as election observers. Observers from the Alliance attended 1,810 polling stations on election day.

They were supplemented by a group of foreign observers, another Salinas reform.

The election was the first national test of Cuauthémoc Cárdenas's PRD, as well as an important opportunity for the PAN. Cárdenas foundered early on in the campaign. Looking stiff and distant, he attracted little support as the campaign progressed. He was also hurt by his association with the EZLN, which by election day did not have broad popular support in Mexico. His treatment in the press was relatively mixed. Journalists on the radio and in periodicals were relatively balanced in their reporting of the campaign, but television reporters, and particularly Jacobo Zabludovsky at Televisa, attacked Cárdenas mercilessly.

PAN candidate Diego Fernández de Cevallos fared somewhat better in the media. Fernández was a powerful campaigner and a skilled speaker, and by most accounts beat both Cárdenas and Zedillo handily in Mexico's first ever presidential debates in May, which were watched by 40 million people. And then, at the height of the campaign, he dropped out of sight for a month. Given his momentum at the time, many believed that Fernández had been paid off by the Zedillo campaign.

Seventy-eight percent of registered voters went to the polls in the August 21 election, casting 35 million votes (more than 20 percent higher than in 1988). Zedillo's campaign, which focused on the fear that a PRI loss would lead to chaos, won 50.1 percent of the vote, to 26.2 percent for Fernández de Cevallos, and 17 percent for Cárdenas. In the Congress the PRI lost twenty deputies.

In the weeks before the election the PRI engaged in a series of traditional abuses, vote-buying, pressing their allies in the media to slant their coverage, and manipulating the process, though on election day poll observers through much of the country alleged only a minimum of fraud. The worst abuses seem to have taken place in the Chiapas highlands, where the EZLN and other groups complained of widespread fraud in the federal and state elections, both of which were won by the PRI. Others grumbled about dirty tricks, and the alleged secret deal between the PRI and PAN, but many Mexicans came out of the August elections with a hope that normalcy was returning.

The promise of a return to normalcy proved short lived. On September 28, José Francisco Ruiz Massieu, former governor of Guerrero and then secretary-general of the PRI, was gunned down on a busy street as he left a breakfast meeting in a downtown Mexico City restaurant. The gunman, Daniel Aguilar Treviño, was captured at the scene, and under torture by police he named several accomplices, including Carlos Cantú Narváez and Fernando Rodriguez Gonzalez. In turn Rodriguez Gonzalez implicated his boss, Tamaulipas congressman Manuel Muñoz Rocha, a close associate of the president's brother, Raúl Salinas. Muñoz Rocha disappeared the following day (September 29), but not before making several calls to Raúl Salinas's home. Raúl, and by extension Carlos, seemed to lie at the heart of the case.

Mexican law forbids judicial officials from investigating the deaths of close family members, but Carlos Salinas immediately named Mario Ruiz Massieu, José Francisco's brother and attorney general in charge of federal drug investigations, as the special prosecutor in the case. Mario quickly cleared Raúl, but beyond this he did not last long as special prosecutor. He resigned on November 23, just days before Zedillo's inauguration claiming that high government officials, including attorney general Humberto Benitez Treviño, were obstructing his investigation. In a further bizarre turn, he declared that he had three boxes of evidence implicating the right wing of the PRI in the murder. His resignation left Mexicans with a collage of conspiracy theories, as the aura of political transparency and clean government was shattered. A month later it would be the myth of economic stability which would prove hollow, as the last façade of salinastroika collapsed.

The peso crisis

One of the hallmarks of the Salinas presidency was a stable currency, and even in the political crises of 1994 he could defend his administration by noting this achievement. A stable currency promoted foreign investment, helped keep inflation low, and contributed to a gradual increase in the standard of living of Mexicans of all social classes. Salinas allowed the peso to fluctuate within a fairly narrow range by selling dollars when the peso was falling, and buying dollars when the peso rose to a level where it threatened to make Mexican exports too expensive to compete on the international market. As long as Mexico maintained a healthy supply of foreign reserves to fund these currency manipulations, this policy was viable. Reserves grew steadily after 1988, and were $29 billion in February 1994.

The size of Mexico's foreign reserve holdings masked a series of long-term problems. After several years of economic growth, Mexicans were buying more and more consumer goods from the US, and contracting a growing debt to foreign creditors. Mexican banks were over-extended, having borrowed heavily to finance local loans, but were beginning to have trouble meeting their obligations because significant numbers of their loans were either in default or close to defaulting (illegal loans were also a significant problem). Debts accumulated by the banks and consumers were exacerbated by the fact that the government's industrial development model required significant imports of technology and components (which were then assembled and re-exported), which in turn did little to help the current account deficit. In short, Mexico was importing more than it was exporting.

These problems were made worse by Salinas's relatively fixed exchange rate. Under most circumstances, the growing debt and trade imbalance would cause the peso to lose value, a process that over time would tend to correct the trade imbalance. Because Salinas was so committed to a stable currency, however, this was not an option. In effect, by maintaining a stable currency, he was actually making the currency appreciate in value, and in order to do this Salinas needed to prop up the currency by selling dollars and buying pesos. This strategy was risky because as foreign reserves were used to prop up the currency, the country was left more vulnerable to insolvency should investors chose to move their money out of the Mexican economy.

Salinas tried to counteract the danger of capital flight by issuing a growing portion of Mexico's debt in *tesobonos*, bonds that were pegged to the US dollar and kept investors safe from potential devaluations. The problem with the *tesobono* was that any downward pressures on the currency would make them extremely costly to the government, which collected its revenue in pesos but would have to repay its creditors in dollars. The *tesobonos* were also a short-term bond; investors were repaid with interest every few months. As long as those investors who held *tesobonos* were willing to trade their old bonds for new ones, this was not a problem, but if these investors began to fear for the solvency of the Mexican government, and cashed out their investments, the Mexican government would go into default if their foreign reserves could not cover the debt.

Each of the crises of 1994 – the Zapatista uprising, the assassinations of Colosio and Ruiz Masseiu, and even the election – put pressure on Mexico's foreign reserves, as investors took their capital out of the Mexican economy and drew down the surplus. Foreign reserves were also hurt when, in early 1994, the US Federal Reserve raised interest rates in the US, drawing dollars out of Mexico and into the US economy. The Mexican government soon began encountering problems in its efforts to finance the current account deficit, and by mid-year Mexico was facing a liquidity crisis. At this point Salinas had two choices: he could either devalue the peso or raise interest rates. He chose the latter, and supplemented this by offering even more *tesobonos*. Over time devaluation became a more pressing concern, but Salinas refused to consider this option. US foreign exchange holdings remained around $17 billion until November, but the value of *tesobonos* increased from $3.1 billion in March to $12.6 billion in November. This amounted to a dollarization of Mexico's internal debt, and was made worse by the fact that dollar inflows into the country did not come back after the election. Toward the end of the year it looked as if Mexico's 1994 current account deficit would be $30 billion.

In the early 1990s current account deficits were financed by foreign investment, but these capital flows were volatile. The billions in speculative investment that flowed into Mexico during the Salinas administration could be pulled out with a simple keystroke. Salinas knew that devaluation might lead to a massive outflow of capital, because most foreign investors in Mexico were not long-term, value investors, but individuals who came into Mexico with fears about institutional stability, and who would probably rush out of the market at the slightest sign of trouble. He was thus faced with a series of unappealing options. Dwindling foreign exchange holdings suggested that the peso needed to be devalued, but devaluation would likely cause more capital flight.

As Salinas dawdled, the treasury had several bad days in October and November, culminating on Friday November 18, when $1.65 billion in foreign reserves were pulled out of the country in a single day. Salinas's advisors recommended that he increase the band within which the peso fluctuated by 15 percent in order to deal with the crisis, but he refused. As a result, by the time Zedillo assumed the presidency on December 1 foreign reserves had fallen to $12.5 billion. Much to his surprise, he also found that during 1994 the government had issued $25 billion in short-term bonds. During the year *tesobonos* had grown from 3 percent of foreign debt to 40 percent. The treasury did not have the resources to meet its obligations.

On December 19 Marcos falsely claimed that the EZLN had occupied thirty-eight villages in Chiapas, a public relations stunt that gave Zedillo the cover he needed to announce on the following day that he was increasing the band of peso fluctuation by 15 percent. He probably imagined that the administration could blame any financial instability on the EZLN, though he underestimated the response by Mexico's debt holders. Wall Street traders were enraged that Zedillo's finance minister, Jaime Serra Puche, informed Mexican traders before he told Wall Street about the change, and the following day $4 billion worth of investments were withdrawn from the country. This left only $6 billion in reserves, not nearly enough to meet the government's obligations. On December 22 Serra was forced to freeze wages and prices for sixty days, and float the peso, whereupon it dropped by 20 percent. Within weeks Mexico would see a wave of public protests, and the peso would fall to 5.35 to the dollar.

The impact on Mexicans was immediate. Unofficial prices jumped and working people experienced severe economic problems. Having become more deeply in debt than ever before – car loans, credit cards, and floating mortgages – middle-class families were devastated. During 1995 the peso lost half its value and the GDP contracted by 6 percent, the worst single-year drop since the Great Depression. Interest rates peaked at 80 percent in March, and nation-wide employment fell by over 8 percent. The inflation rate for the year was 52 percent, contributing to a drop in real wages of 20 percent. Zedillo weathered the storm without a generalized insurrection, but 1994, and for that matter 1995, did not seem to bode well either for the future of the PRI or the future of globalization in Mexico.

Rural rebellion, political assassinations, and financial crisis marked Mexico's first year as a partner in NAFTA. Given the temporal link between these phenomena, we might be tempted to believe that they were linked in a causal relationship. One argument might go: NAFTA caused the Zapatista rebellion, which in turn cascaded into political assassinations, economic volatility, increasing vulnerability to the vagaries of the global marketplace, and ultimately economic disaster. This is an appealing way to organize the story, but it risks imposing coherence on the events of 1994 that may not be warranted. To be sure, when we examine each of these phenomena we can draw out ways in which they were conditioned by Mexico's emerging place in the global economy, yet each of the disasters of 1994 spoke of very specific local histories, practices, and trajectories. Indeed, the Chiapas rebellion conditioned larger political and economic crises during the year, but each of these problems did not derive from Chiapas. Rather, they took the form that they did because they followed the uprising. The same could be said of NAFTA. NAFTA conditioned each of these crises, but can we really say with certainty that NAFTA caused them? Such a claim seems foolhardy.

These questions go to the heart of any effort to understand the history of Mexico and globalization. The following chapters will take up each of the themes that characterized Mexico's "year of living dangerously," always endeavoring to find the balance between an analysis that is rooted in the local and one that is rooted in the global. The value of this approach is that it reminds us that globalization has not obliterated or standardized specific local experiences. Rather, global phenomena are invariably refracted through local practices and histories, producing a series of distinct stories of the global era.

4 | The last days of the PRI?

Ernesto Zedillo spent most of his adult life as a relatively anonymous government official before being catapulted into the spotlight in March 1994. During the campaign he came across as an uncharismatic technocrat, and many believed he was simply a puppet for Carlos Salinas. In the early days of 1995, with the economy in free-fall, scandals multiplying, and renewed conflict in Chiapas, Mexicans could have been forgiven for thinking that he was not the man to steer the nation away from the abyss. They could also have been forgiven for predicting, perhaps a little too enthusiastically, that they were witnessing the dying gasps of the PRI.

The PRI offered many good reasons to believe this. After a dozen years of technocratic rule, characterized by economic liberalization, trade agreements, and a slow erosion of the traditional vote-buying capacity of the state and party, old-style *priistas* (the dinosaurs) used the cover of the peso crisis to go into open revolt. Globalization and democratic openings were destroying the traditional mechanisms they used to hold on to power, and they believed they needed to rescue their party before it was too late. Just weeks after taking power Zedillo failed in his attempt to force Roberto Madrazo, the fraudulently elected PRI governor of Tabasco, to step down. Madrazo refused to accept a deal Zedillo brokered to allow an opposition candidate, Andrés Manuel López Obrador, to take over as governor, and even stormed and physically occupied the statehouse. All the while he openly attacked the technocrats, and called for the party to rediscover its populist roots. Documents later made public revealed that Madrazo spent $38.8 million on the governor's race, thirty-three times the limit allowed. Even so, Madrazo was powerful enough to avoid prosecution.

Madrazo was a member of the old-boy network in the PRI. His father was a former governor.[1] He was a former leader of the National

PRI youth, and a protégé of Carlos Hank González (*el profesor*), who had amassed an enormous fortune while serving as a public official. Products of a party that had always used its control of federal and state resources to hold on to power, *priistas* like Madrazo believed that fraud, threats, violence, and investigations of opponents were reasonable means of maintaining PRI hegemony. Moreover, pressure from within the PRI, including a campaign organized by *el profesor* to defend Madrazo, showed Zedillo that the dinosaurs were still quite formidable.

Zedillo lost his battle with Madrazo, but his next move showed that he would not bow down to the power brokers in the PRI. On February 28 he arrested Raúl Salinas on suspicion of conspiring with PRI congressman Manuel Muñoz Rocha to assassinate José Francisco Ruiz Massieu (Muñoz Rocha, a close ally of Salinas, had gone missing around the time of the murder). Raúl had played a minor public role in the Salinas administration, remaining in the background as the Mexican press and foreign observers fawned over the miracles performed by his brother. It was only in early 1995 that he began to assume a much larger profile, eventually emerging as a powerful symbol of the excesses of his brother's administration. Over the next several years Raúl would be connected to dozens of tales of corruption, betrayal, and even drugs trafficking, forever linking the Salinas family name to some of the worst examples of abuse of power in Mexican history.

His arrest was unprecedented in all the years of PRI rule in Mexico. Presidents and their families had always been above the law. Two days later Mario Ruiz Massieu was detained and interrogated for eight hours. That evening, after learning that he would be arrested for his part in suppressing evidence in the investigation of his brother's death, he fled to the US. The following day he was arrested at Newark airport for failing to report that he was carrying $46,000 with him as he boarded a flight bound for Spain. The events that followed veered from the disheartening to the surreal.

It was then that Carlos Salinas entered the fray. He had been biding his time since leaving office, quietly campaigning for the director generalship of the WTO, but on March 3 he abruptly left Mexico City for Monterrey, where he went into a neighborhood of low-income housing built by his government, knocked on the door of his friend Rosa Coronado, and asked to stay in her home. He then announced that he was going on a hunger strike, and would not end his protest until Zedillo made it clear to the public that he bore no responsibility for the financial crisis or for obstruction of justice in the Colosio case. He ended his hunger strike after forty-four hours, and flew to Mexico City, where Zedillo agreed to clear him of blame in the peso crisis and the Colosio case. At the same time, Zedillo said nothing about Salinas's role in the Ruiz Massieu case. On March 11 Carlos left the country for New York. For several years he led a peripatetic existence, first in Montreal, and then Ireland (where he would be safe from the possibility of prosecution in Mexico, because Ireland and Mexico had no extradition treaty), before finally returning to Mexico after 2000.

Cleared of official blame, Carlos nevertheless remained the intellectual author of the Colosio assassination in the minds of many Mexicans. In T-shirts that became ubiquitous in Mexico during 1995, he was caricatured as a *chupacabra*, a mythical vampire alien, who had "sucked the blood out of his country." The public image of Salinas only worsened when it was revealed that he had given Mario Ruiz Massieu $120,000 just before he withdrew from his brother's murder investigation, a payment many suspect was linked to a deal to exonerate Raúl or destroy evidence of Carlos's malfeasance. Later PR efforts – including a massive autobiography that offered an almost day-by-day account of his presidency – would only backfire, instilling more public hostility, and alienating his own family members. In his memoir, released in 2000, he also took aim at the sitting president, something that no former president had ever done. Watching these events unfold with evident glee, Carlos Monsivais summed up the feelings of many in the opposition by declaring that "the PRI is dying."

Salinas was disgraced, but he did escape prison. Raúl and Ruiz Massieu were not so lucky. In 1995 evidence mounted that Mario had been involved in both the suppression of evidence in his brother's assassination and a massive money laundering scheme. US officials were particularly interested in an account he controlled at the Texas Commerce Bank, which contained $9,041,598. These funds had been deposited over thirteen months, beginning in December 1993, just after Ruiz Massieu had been put in charge of hunting down drug traffickers. The account was opened with a $40,000 deposit, followed by twenty-four others ranging between $119,500 and $477,320. The deposits were carried into the bank in boxes and suitcases, often filled with $20 bills secured by rubber bands. Ruiz Massieu claimed the monies were the proceeds from real estate transactions, but US officials were not convinced.

In a February 1997 civil trial, the US Department of Justice alleged that the $9 million in the Houston Commerce Bank were proceeds from the drug trade. They noted that under his watch Mexican anti-drug efforts had been a shambles, and that Mario had impeded investigations into drug trafficking and exonerated corrupt police officials. US officials also claimed that Mario had informed the trafficker Juan García Abrego of an impending raid in 1993, after which he opened the bank accounts in Houston. These allegations helped to explain his resignation on November 23, 1994, as he was likely fearful that Antonio Lozano Gracia, Zedillo's choice for attorney general, would uncover his crimes.

US officials made a series of other damning allegations. They claimed that the larger conspiracy included Raúl, Carlos, their sister Adriana and father Raúl Salinas Lozano, along with Luis Donaldo Colosio. Prosecutors presented evidence that Raúl, Carlos, and the Ruiz Massieu brothers had met repeatedly with one of the most important traffickers in the country at a ranch owned by Raúl. Moreover, the US attorney's office also presented testimony by Magdalena Pelayo, who claimed that Luis Donaldo Colosio and José Francisco Ruiz Massieu had stolen significant sums of money originating in the drug trade. This offered a possible explanation for their assassinations.

Ruiz Massieu was convicted of bribe-taking in the civil trial, and forfeited $7.9 million of the money in the Houston Commerce Bank to the US government. He did not go free, however, as the US government placed him under house arrest as it pursued a criminal case for money laundering. On September 15, 1999 he was found dead at his home in New Jersey, an apparent suicide. At the time he faced unresolved charges in the US, and was fighting extradition efforts by the Mexican government on corruption charges. His suicide note blamed Zedillo for his brother's and his own death. Rumors circulating at the time of his death suggested that Mario was on the verge of cooperating with US authorities.

Every time Raúl's name came up in these cases, there was a renewed outburst of public opprobrium toward the Salinas brothers in Mexico. It was not so much that Raúl had used his position as a top official in Mexico's government food agency to amass a fortune (he was known as "Mister 10 percent"[2]). This was a relatively common practice for Mexican public officials.[3] Public anger was rather a product of the scale of the corruption, which defied even normal expectations of graft, and bitterness over the economic collapse of 1994. Raúl was the poster child for the excesses of the Salinas regime, and an ideal target if Zedillo wanted to distance himself from the previous administration.

Raúl's arrest in the Ruiz Massieu case was based on the testimony of Fernando Rodríguez González. Rodríguez González did not name Salinas in his first confession, overseen by Mario Ruiz Massieu. Pablo Chapa Bezanilla, the second prosecutor in the case, convinced Rodríguez González to implicate Raúl as the conspiracy leader in part by paying him $500,000. Perhaps seeking to improve his negotiating power, later in 1995 Rodríguez González changed his story once again, this time throwing Carlos Salinas under the bus. In his third confession he claimed that Ruiz Massieu died only because Carlos Salinas had prevented doctors from giving the proper medical care. Even the gunman changed his story, claiming at one point that he had personally witnessed Raúl's involvement, and telling prosecutors that he had been trained by former US and Mexican military officers.

Things started looking up for Raúl after news of the $500,000 payment was made public, but Chapa's case against him found new life when on October 9, 1996 a clairvoyant who worked for Raúl, Francisca Zetina, led investigators to a body on Raúl's ranch in the western suburbs of Mexico City. The attorney general was ecstatic about the discovery, and immediately indicated that he believed it to be the body of the missing congressman, Muñoz Rocha. The evidence, however, was far from convincing, and within weeks it became clear that the body had been planted. Chapa and Lozano were fired on December 2, 1996 for trying to suppress forensic evidence in the case, and Chapa quickly left the country, with prosecutors on his heels. Investigators then revealed that the body belonged to a cousin of the clairvoyant, who had died accidentally some time before, and that she had hatched the entire plot while being paid $150,000 by Chapa as an informant. Zetina, six of her relatives, and María Bernal (Raúl's former mistress) were imprisoned for planting the body.

The case then fell to the new attorney general, Jorge Madrazo Cuéllar. He appointed José Luis Ramos Rivera to prosecute the case. With little untainted evidence left, he built his case around the testimony of Rodríguez González. It was thus surprising to many that on January 21, 1999 Raúl Salinas was convicted by federal judge Ricardo Ojeda Bohórquez of ordering the assassination of Ruiz Massieu and sentenced to fifty years in prison (reduced to twenty-seven on appeal). He was also convicted of perjury and the use of false documents, but acquitted of tax fraud. Critical to the conviction was evidence that several members of the assassination team tried to contact Raúl in the days following Ruiz Massieu's assassination. The judge also relied on testimony by Fernando and Jorge Rodríguez González, who claimed that they had been tortured by investigators working for Mario and forced to retract comments implicating Raúl in their early police statements. In one final twist, the judge in the case held that Raúl ordered the assassination in part because of his bitterness about Massieu's divorce from his sister Adriana a decade earlier.[4]

There was no direct evidence of Raúl's role, and the conviction was based principally on the testimony of clearly biased witnesses, which led to an immediate appeal by Salinas's lawyers. The magazine *Proceso*, not known for its sympathy to the PRI, called the verdict "suspect," and it was publicly denounced even by family members of Ruiz Massieu. Critics were particularly troubled by the fact that Fernando Rodríguez González offered multiple versions of the events surrounding the assassination over ten depositions, by the money he received from the attorney general, and by the special-treatment and coaching he received from prosecutors. Wholesale changes in testimony by other witnesses also fueled suspicions of impropriety.

Raúl remained in Almoloya prison for ten years (though, in accordance with the surreal nature of the crime, many Mexicans believed he was not really in prison), but was freed on bail of $2.96 million on June 14, 2005, after his murder conviction was overturned. Charges of illicit enrichment are still pending in Mexico, though given the time he has already served it is unlikely that he will return to prison.

The other kind of global trade

It may seem surprising that to this date the conviction that has eluded Mexican officials in the Salinas case is one for illicit enrichment. Since 1995 a great deal of evidence has surfaced that Raúl acquired hundreds of millions of dollars illicitly while his brother was president. He opened a series of bank accounts under false names, beginning in 1989, and between 1991 and 1994 Raúl worked through Citibank's private banking unit to launder at least $90 million dollars into Swiss accounts. During this time his official salary was less than $200,000 per year.

In October 1998 Swiss officials seized more than $90 million in assets in accounts linked to Raúl (the total would later climb to $130 million), claiming they were ill-gotten gains from protection he had offered to drug traffickers. Their decision was based in part on the testimony of eighty witnesses who claimed they had seen Salinas meet with traffickers and facilitate their relationships with high government officials. Swiss officials estimated that Salinas's total take from traffickers' bribes was in excess of $500 million.

Mexican officials also froze $119 million in accounts controlled by Raúl, but have failed thus far to convict him of illicit enrichment because Salinas claims that the money came from an investment fund he was managing for associates. When Swiss officials froze the accounts, Carlos Peralta Quintero filed suit in a Mexican court demanding $49.7 million from Salinas that he claimed he had invested with him in 1994. Peralta Quintero, who had won a valuable license from the government to set up a cell phone company in 1993, claimed he had "invested" $50 million in a joint venture with Raúl, for which he had no paperwork. Others also allegedly invested monies in Raúl's ventures, including Ricardo Salinas Pliego, who acquired TV Azteca in 1993 in murky circumstances, and then "lent" Raúl $25 million. These claims, though open to allegations of a different kind of corruption, had the effect of explaining much of the money confiscated in Switzerland. Partly owing to this Raúl has never been indicted in the US on drug charges.[5]

The case gained new life in late 2000, when in a conversation with his sister taped at Almoloya, Raúl alleged that his brother had provided him with false passports and huge sums of cash, proceeds from bribes he received in the privatization process. Salinas knew that the conversation would be taped, and made these allegations only after his brother publicly called him to account for his ill-gotten gains. Investigators later concluded that Raúl transferred $38 million out of Carlos's presidential accounts and into his own accounts, and then sent the money abroad. The charges of illicit enrichment that are now pending came out of these revelations.

Nevertheless, if indeed the sums deposited in Switzerland exceeded $500 million, the only reasonable explanation for the money is that, in addition to accepting bribes in exchange for political favors, Raúl Salinas was deeply involved in protecting drug traffickers. Raúl hardly stands alone among his contemporary officials. In recent years evidence has come to light connecting a large number of officials to the drug trade. The former director of the Federal Judicial Police, Adrián Carrera Fuentes, was convicted and sentenced to six years in prison in June 1998 on charges of money laundering on behalf of traffickers (he was later released because of testimony he provided in the Mario Ruiz Massieu case). On April 5, 1999, the governor of Quintana Roo, Mario Villanueva, disappeared amid accusations that he protected traffickers and laundered money. He now stands accused of receiving $30 million for protecting the shipment of cocaine to the US. Villanueva is currently awaiting trial in Almoloya prison, and is the subject of an extradition request by US officials, who charge that he facilitated the shipment of 200 tons of cocaine to the US when he was governor between 1993 and 1999. Mexican officials allegedly knew about his involvement in the drug trade as early as 1997.[6]

More spectacular is the case of General Jesús Gutiérrez Rebollo, once Mexico's top official in charge of drug enforcement. He was arrested for working for the drug traffickers on February 18, 1997, just one week after being publicly praised by Clinton administration officials. Gutiérrez Rebollo had been credited with capturing several major figures in the cocaine trade, but it turned out he had been attacking one cartel while allowing another to work unhindered by law enforcement. More than this, he put the military – arms, soldiers, transport – at their disposal. In an ironic twist, he was arrested because he asked a drug trafficker to arrange for an apartment for his mistress in Mexico City after he was appointed drug tsar. She wound up living in a domicile owned by the leader of the Juárez cartel, and by extension so did the general. He was convicted in early 1998 on drugs and arms charges, and sentenced to forty years in prison. A month later his lawyer, Tomás Arturo González Velázquez, was assassinated as he sat in his car in Guadalajara.

Gutiérrez Rebollo's conviction came in the midst of a major transformation in Mexico's status in the international drug trade. Mexico began exporting limited amounts of heroin and marijuana to the US in the 1930s, and Mexican officials have a long history of taking bribes to protect growers and traffickers. This remained a relatively small-scale endeavor until the 1970s, when the Colombian cartels started moving a large volume of Andean cocaine through Mexico. Mexican officials took full advantage of the opportunities this new trade represented, and by the early 1980s the 1,500 agents of the Federal Security Agency (DFS) acted as a critical source of protection for traffickers. Their entire effort was coordinated through the DFS chief, José Antonio Zorillo. This arrangement collapsed only after a member of the DFS was directly involved in the assassination of US Drug Enforcement Administration (DEA) agent Enrique Camarena. Several, including Zorrilla, were eventually jailed, and the DFS was disbanded. Left without legitimate jobs but with an intimate knowledge of the drug trade, many former agency members became directly involved in trafficking.

In the late 1980s Mexican traffickers began taking their payment from the Colombians in cocaine rather than cash, and were able to generate massive profits as they expanded to new markets in the western US. As the American appetite for drugs grew, and law enforcement efforts worked to keep prices high, a growing number of Mexican groups competed for a share in the potential profits from the drug trade. Four loosely organized cartels vied for the Mexican narcotics trade (mostly in cocaine, marijuana, and heroin). These included the Juárez cartel, headed by Amado Carrillo Fuentes, the Gulf cartel, headed at first by Juan García Abrego (and after his arrest and deportation to the US, by Oscar Malherbe de León), the Sinaloa/Jalisco cartel, led by Hector Luis Palma-Salazar, and the Tijuana cartel, ruled by the Arrellano-Felix brothers (Benjamín, Javier, Ramón, and Francisco). By the late 1990s, 60 percent of the cocaine and at least half of the marijuana and meta-amphetamine imported into the US came from Mexico. This allowed Mexican gangs to earn between $17 and $30 billion per year. In turn, they paid about $500 million in bribes annually.

One of the key actors in these developments was Amado Carillo Fuentes. He was known as the *señor del cielo* (the man of the skies) because he bought Boeing 727s, loaded them with up to 6 tons of cocaine, and then flew them from Colombia to Northern Mexican airfields, where he offloaded the drugs and smuggled them into the US. Carillo Fuentes used military airfields, and often simply abandoned the planes after they arrived in Mexico because he could earn $100 million in a single flight. These brazen practices required millions in bribes to a network of judges, prosecutors, politicians, and police, including Mario Villanueva and Jesús Gutiérrez Rebollo. Carillo Fuentes seemed untouchable until the arrest of Gutiérrez Rebollo, which put him in a national spotlight. At first he tried to bribe his way out of trouble, but in the end he sent his family to Chile and underwent plastic surgery in a Mexico City clinic on July 3, 1997. He allegedly died the following day, owing to a reaction between hepatitis, drugs in his system, and the anesthetic used during the surgery. One of his doctors immediately fled the country for the US and was given protection in the US Witness Protection Program in return for information on the Juárez cartel. The doctor in charge of the operation, Dr Jaime Godoy Singh, was assassinated shortly thereafter. On November 2, 1997 his body was found stuffed inside a cement-filled barrel by a roadside in Guerrero.

In the months after Carillo Fuentes's death, a battle over control of the Juárez trade led to dozens of deaths, which in turn were part of a much larger trend. As the profits from the drug trade escalated, so too did the violence in the regions where the cartels based their business. In the Yucatán, Tijuana, Juarez, and Guadalajara, battles over control of the cartels could leave dozens dead in killing sprees.[7] Judges could be bribed, and police enlisted in the violence or intimidated into silence, allowing the traffickers to kill with impunity.

Drug traffickers could also depend on the passivity of journalists to keep their deeds out of the public eye, and even adopted the PRI's traditional practice of paying journalists up to several hundred dollars per week to remain silent about the drug trade (some drug traffickers even acquired control of newspapers). Those who refused to go along paid a heavy price. Jesús Blancornelas, editor of *Zeta*, and a regular critic of the drug traffickers, has been the victim of repeated assassination attempts by traffickers, and currently has an $80,000 bounty on his head. He was severely wounded in a 1997 assassination attempt that left his bodyguard dead. In that attack Blancornelas's car was hit 180 times, and he was hit four times. His bodyguard was shot thirty-eight times. In the same year three other prominent journalists were killed.

The most dangerous city in the world

Mexicans had little faith that their justice system could handle these crimes, in part because at the very moment that drug violence exploded, the police and judicial system seemed to reach their nadir. By the mid-1990s, Mexico City was gaining a reputation as one of the most dangerous places in the world. In part fueled by the lawlessness of the drug trade, and in part fueled by the economic crisis, violent crime in Mexico skyrocketed.

Kidnappings were a particular favorite for a growing network of criminal organizations. In 1995 alone there were 1,500 kidnappings in Mexico, with victims ranging from the very wealthy to unlucky members of the working class caught in the wrong place at the wrong time. Kidnappings for ransom multiplied, and kidnappers secured millions in ransom from businessmen and public officials for the release of family members. Far more common, however, were the more mundane attacks in which members of armed gangs would briefly hijack a bus in search of a quick score. Also common were taxi kidnappings, in which an unsuspecting victim hailed a cab and was either robbed immediately or held for several hours so that their bank accounts could be emptied. Stories multiplied of individuals who were kidnapped in mid-afternoon, forced to make a withdrawal from an ATM, and then held until after midnight, so that another withdrawal could be made. Most victims escaped with their lives, but reports of people killed in these crimes seemed to appear in the newspapers on an almost daily basis.

Over time it became clear that rather than preventing these crimes, the police were in fact committing many of them. One report in 1997 suggested that police or former police officers committed more than half the crimes in Mexico City. As part of an increasingly sophisticated crime network, police used their computers and data-bases to create systematic extortion and kidnapping rackets. These practices came to light after a wave of kidnappings in Morelos in 1994, when the head of the state's anti-kidnapping agency was con-victed of protecting and aiding kidnappers. His successor, Armando Martínez Salgado, was arrested in January 1998 with the body of a seventeen-year-old kidnap victim in his car. Forty officers from his unit were fired, and the scandal led to the arrests of the state attorney general and state police chief in 1999. More notorious still was Daniel Arizmendi, a former police officer with a vast protection network that allowed him to escape discovery while carrying out more than twenty kidnappings, for which he collected millions in ransom money. His signature tactic involved cutting an ear off his hostage and sending it to the victim's family along with his ransom demand. He was arrested in August 1998.

What caused the jump in violent crime? One could contend that it seemed worse than it was; that part of the problem was simply the result of better information flows. Indeed, something like 50 percent of the crime in Mexico City still goes unreported. Other explanations point to a number of factors related to Mexico's changed global relationships. Drug traffickers certainly prompted crime waves, not only tied to drugs themselves but through a proliferation of weapons in Mexico. Drug trafficking also corrupted police agencies, making other crimes less likely to be solved. Beyond all this were the discour-aging statistics on poverty and employment that Mexicans faced after

1994. Poor people not only grew more desperate in the mid-1990s, they also watched bitterly as Mexico's middle and upper classes prospered. As the gaps widened, and the poor felt the symbolic violence of wage freezes and unemployment, they became less likely to sympathize when wealthy Mexicans were the victims of actual violence. In fact, poor people sometimes perpetrated that violence as a part of their survival strategies.

One could be forgiven for watching the crises in the PRI, the spectacular drugs trials, and the waves of violence in the 1990s and concluding that Mexico was coming unglued. Mexico City became a noticeably more anxious place in the latter part of the decade, as the middle and upper classes (along with foreign residents) purchased armored cars, hired bodyguards, and increasingly secluded themselves in gated communities. Poor people also experienced a growing anxiety about violence. They too were victims of kidnappings, violence on buses and in the metro, and omnipresent police corruption.

And yet Mexico did not sink into chaos in the midst of these crises. In part this may have been because Mexicans were already deeply familiar with violence. Mexicans have always had strategies to deal with the violence of everyday life; the rich live in fortresses with broken glass atop their walls, the poor avoid the police at all costs. Likewise, even if they were struck by the extremes of corruption in the Salinas administration, Mexicans were not particularly surprised to learn that their public officials had enriched themselves while in office. What surprised, even shocked, most Mexicans was that it was becoming more difficult for high-ranking public officials to get away with their ill-gotten gains. No ex-president since Plutarco Elías Calles in the 1930s had been forced to flee the country. No presidential brother had ever been imprisoned, and Mexicans had never seen as many public officials arrested as they saw in the years between 1994 and 2000.

Ernesto Zedillo was largely responsible for each of these developments. Knee-jerk opponents of the PRI and EZLN sympathizers often demonize Zedillo as a neo-liberal economist, an abuser of human rights who ratcheted up the violence in Mexico, especially in Chiapas. His supporters counter that he was singularly important in an effort to expose drug dealing, corruption, and violence in Mexico, and that his efforts laid the groundwork for profound transformations in Mexico's civic life. They claim that Mexico's democratic openings – and the death of the old PRI – had as much to do with his efforts as they did with those of any other person.

Zedillo versus the PRI

Born into a working-class family in Mexico City but raised in the border city of Mexicali, Zedillo was a classic outsider in a profoundly insular political system. He relied on government scholarships to obtain his education at the National Polytechnic Institute and Yale (where he earned a PhD in Economics in 1978), and was not part of the inner circle of *priistas* during most of his career. He lacked a close cohort of colleagues and supporters, and likely never aspired to be president before those fateful events in March 1994. This perhaps explains why, in January 1995, he invited leaders of all the major political parties to Los Pinos to begin negotiations for a complete overhaul of the political system.

These meetings produced a significant legislative agenda in 1995 and 1996. Bills sponsored by Zedillo gave the IFE more autonomy and reformed the Federal Elections Commission. The government would no longer organize elections, spending limits were established, and parties were promised public funding. The government was also now required to monitor the media to ensure fairness. This last measure would be hard to enforce, and risked stifling free speech, but was welcomed by opposition parties, which had suffered constant and often false attacks from the TV networks since the 1988 election.

Zedillo also tried to depoliticize and strengthen the justice system. He named PAN lawyer Antonio Lozano Gracia as attorney general. He retired all twenty-five Supreme Court justices, reducing the court to eleven. Under the reformed system judges had to be confirmed by a two-thirds majority in Congress, ensuring that opposition parties would have a say in nominations. Further reforms eliminated PRI membership as a requirement for union and government jobs, and opened the mayor's office of Mexico City to popular election. Given voting patterns in the Federal District, this virtually ensured that the PRD (and most likely Cárdenas) would assume one of the most visible elected posts in the country.

None of these reforms was inevitable; each promised to empower the opposition at the expense of the PRI, and could have been avoided or watered down (as some were, including the limits on campaign spending) if Zedillo had taken a different approach to political reform. Even though the PRI was weakened in 1994, it remained the only truly national party, and had such an arsenal of weapons at its disposal that *priistas* could probably have continued to manipulate the system for the foreseeable future (especially if the PAN and PRD split the opposition vote).

Hardliners in the PRI believed that democracy was alien to Mexico. Theirs was the politics of strong leaders, of patronage systems built around the ability to deliver the goods to loyal followers and intimidate troublemakers. In the eyes of the dinosaurs this was the only feasible way to produce a stable political system in Mexico, where the backwardness of most of the population made the notion of universal rights and liberties unthinkable. Moreover, Zedillo sometimes seemed to share these views. He never showed much interest in the human rights of Chiapans, even dramatically increasing the presence of the military in the state in an effort to quell dissent. He was likewise an obvious elitist, lacking the populist touch of his predecessors and acting in an openly condescending manner to his critics, especially if those critics were poor, rural, and Indian.

We would be mistaken, though, to identify his elitism and condescension as empathy with the dinosaurs. Zedillo did not believe in producing stability by maintaining a closely managed hierarchical patronage network; he believed that Mexico's future stability could be guaranteed through adherence to a series of clearly defined values. Free markets, political transparency, and liberal democracy were the answers to Mexico's problems. He was thus an ideological warrior, who believed that market liberalism needed to be accompanied by political liberty, as a matter of principle.

His critics point out that this was an easy position for Zedillo to take, given that he was relatively free of significant political debts (especially after he drove Salinas out of the country), and not closely tied to any of the networks that monopolized political power in

Mexico. More than this, critics contend, the ur-technocrat Zedillo had his attentions focused abroad rather than on Mexico, making him either tone deaf or hostile to those in the PRI who had used nationalism and populism to hold on to power. He wanted to rid Mexico of these anti-democratic tendencies so that the country he governed more closely resembled the country he admired (and where he now makes his home, as the director of the Center for the Study of Globalization at Yale University).

The battle over the gubernatorial election in Tabasco in early 1995 ensured that there would be no love lost between Zedillo and the traditionalists in his party. His relations with the party deteriorated further in 1996, after he eliminated presidential discretionary spending in response to a report by the Civic Alliance[8] that revealed that the president had a $4 billion budget for salaries, and an $86 million discretionary fund for which he did not have to report expenses. These monies had always been used to pay the salaries of thousands of party functionaries, organize support, and buy votes. The presidential slush fund also paid journalists, covered day-to-day party needs, and funded campaigns. When it was eliminated the PRI lost the mechanism that had for generations blurred the line between the party and the state.

Inasmuch as trade liberalization had already weakened the PRI's capacity to protect its political base, Zedillo's reforms further undermined *priista* networks. Like Salinas, Zedillo protected a few vested interests (most notably the PEMEX union), but the combination of anti-labor economic policies and dramatic reductions in the backdoor cash flow created considerable problems for the CTM,[9] long a critical source of support for the PRI. Lacking their traditional means of maintaining loyalty, the CTM began losing members to the rival National Union of Workers (UNT). Union reformers also pushed for democratization within their syndicates, a process that risked undermining the remaining links between the party and one of its traditional pillars.

It was thus unsurprising that Zedillo's reforms caused a near-riot at the PRI Party Congress in 1996. For one brief moment delegates at the congress appeared ready to physically attack Zedillo, and while he managed to avoid violence, the delegates did get their revenge by passing legislation that made it impossible for technocrats to receive the party's nomination for president in the future. The reformed rules set two new requirements for anyone who aspired to the nomination: they must have been a member of the party for at least ten years, and they must have held elected office in the past. Neither Zedillo nor Salinas would have qualified for the nomination under these rules.

Priistas also tried to ignore Zedillo's mandates at the regional level. The president could work with the PAN and PRD to press for reforms in national elections, and could count on a growing number of international NGOs to ensure transparency in the federal process. In local and state elections, however, which were too numerous and generally not glamorous enough to attract international attention, *priistas* had a freer hand to practice business as usual. Given the stakes of local elections – municipal councils and state governments controlled a considerable share of federal funds, and state governments could protect *priistas* from prosecution for past and present crimes – *priistas* often used whatever means they had at their disposal to hold on to power.

Some of the worst political abuses of these years were seen in Guerrero, one of the most violent and corrupt PRI strongholds in the country. On June 28, 1995, police detained and then killed seventeen members of the Southern Sierra Peasant Organization (OCSS) in Aguas Blancas, Guerrero, as they traveled to a demonstration in Atoyac de Álvarez. Witnesses claimed that the police simply ordered the peasants out of their trucks and massacred them, but in response to these claims, Governor Rubén Figueroa released a videotape that showed a peasant aiming a gun at police. He and his police chief claimed that this was clear evidence that the peasants had shot at the police, and that the police responded in self-defense. Figueroa probably believed that the matter was closed. After all, in the two years surrounding the incident more than a hundred members of the opposition had been killed in Guerrero, with no repercussions for the PRI.

The following day the newspaper *El Sol* in Acapulco published two different photos of a single victim of the massacre. The discrepancies between the photos seemed to indicate that the police had planted a gun on the victim. The response from opposition parties was immediate. PRD lawyer Samuel del Villar and members of the National Commission for Human Rights (CNDH) immediately traveled to Guerrero to interview witnesses and gather evidence. The testimony they gathered, coupled with the evidence of a cover-up, was enough to force the government of Guerrero to bring charges against four state officials and twenty of the state's riot police in January 1996. Governor Figueroa pronounced that this was a lamentable case of the local police losing control, and declared the case closed.

This might have been the end of the story if not for the fact that in February 1996 Ricardo Rocha, the host of a popular investigative program on Televisa, received an unedited version of the police tape from an unidentified source. Aired on February 26, the twenty-minute tape showed the massacre in all its brutality. Viewers saw police forcing unarmed peasants from their vehicles and opening fire. The fact that the tape was shown was itself remarkable. A network owned by long-time PRI insiders (the Azcárraga family) revealed a vast cover-up, forcing the Mexican president to watch events unfold on television, just like everyone else. The tape was also the clearest possible evidence of Figueroa's role in covering up the crime. On March 4 Zedillo, who had up to this point remained on the sidelines, sent a request to the Mexican Supreme Court that they investigate human rights violations in the case. Figueroa responded by ordering mass demonstrations of support, trucking in demonstrators from all over the state. This move only further enraged Zedillo, who forced Figueroa to resign under the threat of federal prosecution on March 12.

Zedillo succeeded against Figueroa in 1996 where he had failed in efforts to force Madrazo out as governor of Tabasco in 1995 because by then he had new tools that could be used in his struggles with the PRI. He could rely on a reformed Supreme Court, which in April would conclude that the incident at Aguas Blancas was a premeditated massacre by police, and declare that Figueroa was responsible for egregious human rights violations. The unanimous ruling by the court found that Figueroa undertook a "shocking and coarse" conspiracy to cover up the massacre. The court left it to Zedillo as to whether or not he would prosecute Figueroa, an option that Zedillo ultimately declined. The very possibility that Figueroa might have been prosecuted was enough to force his resignation, and meant that the era of complete impunity for the state-level PRI was effectively over.

Of course, this would not have happened but for the photographs published in *El Sol*, and the tape shown on Televisa. The use of the videotape in the Figueroa case brings to mind other moments in which small, hand-held cameras have shattered the claims made by the powerful; the Rodney King beating in Los Angeles on March 3, 1991 being perhaps the most famous case. The results of exposure on videotape are never a foregone conclusion – lest we forget, Rodney King's attackers were acquitted in their first trial – but once they find a public outlet they have the capacity to change the political landscape. The immediacy of the visual image, be it a photograph or a videotape, exposes official misdeeds more effectively than any amount of oral testimony. That it was the police themselves who made the tape in this case only adds irony to the tragedy.

In the aftermath, emboldened political parties, human rights organizations, and the courts took on the PRI at all levels. By mid-1996 accusations of fraud in seemingly insignificant municipal elections could derail talks between the national parties.[10] National news organizations increasingly followed these elections closely, making it ever more difficult for *priistas* to engage in business as usual.

Elections

The reformed PRI faced its first significant national tests in the 1997 elections, and the results stunned the old guard. Opposition gains at the state level held up, and in the first ever elections for the mayor of Mexico City, Cuauthémoc Cárdenas won with 47 percent of the vote. The PRI won just 25 percent, and 16 percent of voters chose the PAN. After the 1997 elections 44 percent of Mexicans lived in municipalities ruled by opposition parties, up from none just a decade earlier. Most critically, for the first time since the 1920s, in 1997 the PRI lost its majority in Congress. The PRI won only 238 seats in the 500-seat house. The PRD won 125, the PAN 118, and smaller parties won nineteen.

Congress controlled the federal budget, and *priistas* were unprepared to give up an authority that they saw as their birthright. Party strategists decided to delay the opening of Congress until they could work out what to do, but were stunned when PAN and PRD leaders forged a pact to divide up the plum committee assignments and open the session. Lacking the power to stop the proceedings, the PRI walked out of Congress when Porfirio Muñoz Ledo of the PRD was named majority leader, and Santiago Creel, an independent affiliated with the PAN, was elected as second in rank. The PRI majority in the Senate refused to acknowledge the legitimacy of the new Congress and announced it would boycott its proceedings. Their boycott ended only when Zedillo refused to offer his support, forcing the PRI to accept its minority status.

The PAN was a huge winner in 1997, but the most symbolic of victories went to the generation of 1968, which had long been shut out of national politics and victimized by state terrorism. Among the new representatives of the PRD in the Congress were a significant number of veterans of the 1968 student movement. Other veterans of 1968 took prominent positions in the Mexico City government. For Mexico's political opposition it felt like a glorious coming of age, an opportunity to finally make the PRI account for Tlatelolco.

For this and other reasons, the elections seemed to bode very poorly for the PRI. Having lost control of the budget, the PRI had also lost control of their most important mechanism for maintaining party loyalty. In turn Congress became a disorderly center of political conflict, both on the floor of the chamber and in the streets and plazas surrounding San Lázaro. Shifting coalitions of PRI and PAN deputies managed to pass the occasional pro-business measure, but with their eyes focused on the looming 2000 elections, most of the energies of the Congress were devoted to political blood sport.

The PAN offered an imminent political threat to the PRI, but it was the PRD which *priistas* went after most aggressively, particularly the new mayor of Mexico City. *Priistas* did everything they could to create a mess for the incoming mayor. Republicans in the US complained that Clinton's staffers removed the "W"s from their computer keyboards as they left the White House; in Mexico City the outgoing administration took the computers, the antennas, and the televisions, and destroyed city files. City cars – including police cars – went missing. Incoming Cardenistas could not even find drawers for their desks. When Cárdenas tried to hold a press conference, he discovered that the city did not even own a public address sound system.

After examining the morass that was the city government, Cárdenas could have reasonably concluded that the very decision to allow elections for the mayor of the city was a political set-up, designed to make him look like a poor administrator. The city was deeply in debt, had almost no procedural infrastructure, and was saddled with thousands of absentee jobs, paying people who made no work contribution. Public services were stretched beyond breaking point, and almost 200,000 residents of the city lacked sewerage or water. Hundreds of thousands of crimes were committed in the city every year, and 90 percent remained unsolved. The city had a 22 percent unemployment rate, endemic smog, snarled traffic, and was perpetually on the verge of running out of water.

City regulations were so arcane that any effort to follow them precisely, and thus avoid corruption, would lead to government paralysis. Every public service in the city, from tree trimming to drivers' licenses, to refuse disposal, required a bribe (commonly called a *mordida*, or "little bite"). Police officers, who earned around $700 per month, often demanded bribes in order not to commit crimes. Other low-ranking officials earned similarly dismal salaries, and used bribes to supplement their incomes. These bribes would work their way up a pipeline to the sixteen different delegates who ruled the various sectors of the city, enriching thousands of city employees and making corruption very difficult to fight.

Governing such a city would prove a gargantuan task, and opponents would find many opportunities to assail Cárdenas's reputation. He often came across as imperious and distant as mayor, and his enemies took great delight in laying the city's problems at his feet. When on June 5, 1999 Francisco "Paco" Stanley, one of Mexico's most popular television comics, was ambushed and killed in broad daylight by gunmen as he drove his minivan on a Mexico City thoroughfare, Cárdenas was relentlessly attacked in the media. Television commentators in particular, still deeply in the pockets of the PRI, savaged Cárdenas for his failure to curtail street violence, and the anchorman at TV Azteca demanded Cárdenas's resignation.

These attacks stopped abruptly when prosecutors announced that they had found cocaine on Stanley's body, and reports surfaced linking him to organized crime, but Cárdenas's opponents had already linked the mayor to the epidemic of violence in the city. When he resigned to run for the presidency twenty-one months after being elected, he was a much diminished public figure. In spite of some improvements in streets, public services, pollution, and public housing, he left office with a 41 percent approval rating.

Heading into the 2000 presidential election, Cárdenas had to confront more than just a low approval rating. After a burst of national popularity a dozen years before, he had run a distant third in 1994. Worse still, finding growing numbers of PRD adherents chafed at his leadership, they found that the Party of the Democratic Revolution was not so democratic after all. In fact, the PRI seemed to establish stronger democratic credentials than the PRD in 2000, holding democratic primaries to choose their nominee for the first time ever.

The PRI primaries pitted Roberto Madrazo against Francisco Labastida Ochoa. Labastida was not exactly a technocrat, but was a former cabinet member, and in spite of the fact that Zedillo refused to get involved in the process, most observers believed he was Zedillo's choice. Madrazo, who spent $25 million in state funds on his campaign, was an early favorite among the PRI rank and file because he promised more social spending, relaxed fiscal discipline, and a return to old-style PRI politics. Nevertheless, he was dogged by accusations of political corruption, and not broadly popular among party leaders.

Within the PRI the campaign was quite ugly, as those PRI chiefs loyal to Zedillo blocked Madrazo from gaining access to some of his rallies, and used implicit threats to the news media to ensure that coverage of his campaign was largely negative. One radio talk show host was fired simply for interviewing Madrazo (Felipe Manzanárez of *Good Morning Sinaloa*). Ballot boxes were taken at gunpoint in at least one primary, and in Guerrero competing PRI factions resorted to shoot-outs. In the end, few were surprised that Labastida won the nomination.

Vicente Fox, the PAN's nominee, surprised even his own party by winning the nomination. The imposing Fox (he stood over six foot six in cowboy boots) was not a long-time party leader, having first been elected to public office in 1988, before being elected governor of Guanajuato in 1995. Fox bypassed the traditional party elites, launching a national television campaign to introduce himself to the Mexican electorate in 1997. He made a few missteps at first – his talk about privatizing PEMEX resulted in a wave of criticism – but his calls for an end to corruption, nepotism, and inefficiency, and his reputation for clean government in Guanajuato, won many converts among Mexico's emergent middle class.

Although Labastida could point to a 6.9 percent growth in GDP in 1999 as a sign that the PRI was doing a good job running the country, voters had many reasons to choose an opposition candidate in 2000. Aside from long-simmering resentments over corruption, violence, and mismanagement, during the late 1990s the PRI was heavily criticized for its handling of the economic recovery after 1994, and especially for the bail-out of Mexico's recently reprivatized banks after the peso crisis (for more on this, see Chapter 6). Fox did not promise major increases in social spending, but did at least offer that the long tradition of corruption and insider privilege would come to an end. This appealed to the young, urban voters who had car loans, shopped at Wal-Mart, and resented the PRI kleptocracy as both unfair and a threat to their personal ambitions (they had, after all, lost a great deal in the peso crisis, and unlike the politically connected bankers, they were not rescued). Members of the business community, who likewise felt betrayed by the peso crisis of 1994, also contributed heavily to the Fox campaign. Courting their support, Fox railed against the handling of the crisis but was careful to avoid calling for too much transparency on the bail-out.

Fox built a broad base of support by arguing that whatever reason you had for hating the PRI, he was *the* candidate who could defeat Labastida. In the absence of an opposition coalition (which the PRD and PAN discussed, but quickly discarded), the election came down to the question of which party won the largest plurality, and many Mexicans quite rightly feared that PRD and PAN might simply cancel one another out, leaving a victory for the PRI. Capitalizing on this anxiety, Fox represented himself as strong and commanding, a contrast to the lackluster Cárdenas. By focusing much of his energy on the reasons why Cárdenas could never win the presidency, he positioned himself as the only alternative to the PRI. If voters chose Cárdenas, they were effectively casting their vote for the PRI.

The PRI faced its own challenges. With the IFE spending $1.2 billion to oversee the 2000 election, many time-tested electoral strategies had to be abandoned. Fund-raising became an issue in the election because many of the traditional party supporters in the business sector either sat out the election, or supported the PAN. Whereas in 1994 Carlos Slim convinced thirty businessmen to cough up $750 million for the election, including $50 million alone from Emilio Azcárraga, in 2000 the business sector was more independent of the PRI than ever before, focused on international markets and protected from the traditional power of labor and the state by a transformed economy.

That said, the PRI still had the most extensive political networks in the nation, especially in the countryside. The Labastida campaign made aggressive use of these advantages, most notably the close relationship between the PRI and PEMEX. Over the course of the campaign Rogelio Montemayor Seguy, the director of PEMEX, along with several high-level administrators, arranged for $127 million in contributions from the company to the Labastida and other PRI campaigns. PRI officials used this and other (often illicit) sources of money to dole out cement and tin sheets for roofing in some areas, and chickens in others. The governor of Yucatán, Victor Cervera Pacheco, gave away washing machines, paid for out of the state treasury. In the town of Umán, party workers displayed PRI largesse by making a line of 1,003 washing machines. As the election approached the handouts accelerated. Even though the law mandated that campaigning end before election day, 15,000 bags of rice were found in a PRI warehouse in Durango on the eve of the election. The intended use of the rice was obvious; food handouts were always a critical electoral strategy in the PRI.

Party leaders believed these strategies were more crucial than ever, because their internal polls told them that Fox was leading Labastida. Facing something that they had never imagined possible, the dinosaurs pressed the party to do whatever it took to save the presidency for the PRI. The election of 1988 was not so far in the distant past, and the PRI still controlled most of the state governments and a small majority of the municipalities, not to mention an extensive network of party operatives who could ensure that the results of thousands of local polls went in the party's favor.

And yet, 2000 was much too far removed from 1988 for there to be a repeat of the past. Yes, the PRI could still attempt to buy votes and abuse the campaign laws, but once the polling stations were open the PRI was bound by an entirely new set of constraints. Newspapers, television, NGOs, and the vast network of poll watchers run by the Civic Alliance made it virtually impossible to hide nefarious acts at the polling stations. International observers and journalists also came out in force for the 2000 election, drawn in part by Mexico's growing international profile (on both the left and the right), and by a growing curiosity about whether or not the "perfect dictatorship" might actually fall. Televisa and TV Azteca both had their own independent polls in the 2000 election, and given the level of public scrutiny at the polling stations, they could not ignore the results.

Immediately after the polls closed on July 2, both networks declared Fox the victor by a margin of 8 percent. The size of the margin was surprising to many, as was the fact that he won in crucial working-class neighborhoods in the Federal District, where voters simultaneously voted for the PRD candidate for mayor.[11] Watching the election coverage in Los Pinos, Zedillo pressed the party to concede the election. He was rebuffed by Labastida and the dinosaurs, who began to plot strategy in PRI headquarters.

Aware that their power and livelihoods were at stake, *priistas* throughout the country were ready to do whatever it took to hold on to the presidency. Their efforts were derailed at 11 p.m., when José Woldenberg, the chief of the IFE, went on the air to declare Fox the winner. Immediately afterwards, Labastida took to the podium at PRI headquarters to address the nation, but his address was interrupted by Zedillo, who took to the air from Los Pinos to congratulate Fox on his victory. As their leader put a final stake into the heart of his party, Labastida, party leaders and the PRI rank and file fumed. By contrast, Zedillo seemed quite pleased to have secured his place in history by overseeing the first unimpeachably democratic election in Mexico's history.

The final results gave Fox 42.5 percent of the votes, Labastida 36.1 percent, and Cárdenas 16.64 percent. In the Congress the PRI won 209 seats, the PAN 207 and the PRD fifty-four. In the 128-member Senate the PRI retained sixty, compared to forty-six for the PAN and fifteen for the PRD. State-level elections also favored opposition parties. By the end of 2000 opposition parties controlled eleven of thirty-two statehouses, and almost half of municipalities in the country.

The days following the election were difficult ones for the PRI, which had built a national political system based on the assumption that it would always rule, and had then seen its control of the Congress and the presidency evaporate in the span of three years. The dinosaurs blamed the technocrats, and set about regaining their party and country by reinventing themselves as democratic populists. They were still the largest party in the country, and controlled more political offices than any other, but with so many of their traditional mechanisms for holding on to power lost in political and economic openings, the reinvention of the PRI would not be easy.

5 | Border crossings in an age of terror

When Mexicans surveyed their northern border at the dawn of the new millennium, they saw an odd juxtaposition. The border was more open than ever – allowing an almost unlimited flow of commodities north and south – and yet it was more closed to the movement of humans than it had ever been. NAFTA did make movement across the border relatively easy for rich, professional (and mostly white) people, but for the masses of Mexicans who sought opportunities on *el otro lado*, the border was an increasingly perilous place. Vicente Fox promised that one of his principal goals as president would be to reverse this trend. Migration, he declared, would be one of the defining issues of his *sexenio*. No one could possibly have imagined all the reasons why this would be true.

Mexicans have been migrating to the US in search of opportunities since the nineteenth century. In the early twentieth century, when US immigration laws made migration from Europe and Asia more difficult, Mexico became the principal source of low-wage migrant laborers in US mines, factories, and fields. Immigration officials did not generally try to stem the flow of migrants, as they were critical to the economy, but they nonetheless feared the contagion of "dirty" and "racially inferior" Mexicans. These anxieties isolated Mexicans living in the US, and provided a pretext for expelling migrants during economic downturns.

The first governmental efforts to recruit Mexicans to work in the US came with the Bracero Program, a limited-contract labor system adopted during the First World War.[1] By the mid-1920s more than 100,000 Mexicans crossed the border annually for work, but their position remained tenuous. During economic crises and xenophobic moments, hundreds of thousands of Mexicans were deported (453,000 during the Great Depression). When the labor demands in US fields, factories, and mines recovered, so too would migration.

The deportations of the Great Depression were thus followed by a second Bracero Program, initiated in 1942. During twenty years 4.6 million Mexicans came to work in the US under this program. Migrants were placed in an especially disadvantageous situation by the program – short visas and restrictive work contracts ensured that the visa worker could quickly become an "illegal immigrant." Undocumented workers had to accept even lower wages, and could be summarily deported. Operation Wetback, for example, launched in Texas in 1954, led to the deportation of over 1 million Mexicans.

The Bracero Program ended in 1963, after which the US Immigration and Nationality Act was repeatedly amended in attempts to limit Mexican migration.[2] Nevertheless, legal immigration increased from 38,000 per year in 1964 to 67,000 per year in 1986. Over the same period unauthorized entries into the US increased from 87,000 to 3.8 million a year, a figure that reflected the fact that most migrants returned to Mexico more than once per year. Though most ultimately returned to Mexico, in the twenty years after the end of the Bracero Program nearly 30 million Mexicans entered the US without visas.[3]

The Mexican economy grew steadily between 1940 and 1970, and during this time migration to the US was a steady but relatively minor phenomenon. Migrants provided important income for poor families, but low levels of unemployment and gradually improving conditions in Mexico reduced the pressure to migrate. This began to change in the late 1960s, as rural crises increased the urgency of northward migration, a phenomenon that became a central part of the survival strategies of millions of Mexicans after 1982. After 1986 over a million Mexicans entered the US per year, with net immigration of about 400,000. In turn, the waves of Mexican migrants fleeing economic problems at home set off new anxieties in the US. At the height of the crisis, President Reagan famously lamented that the US had "lost control" of its borders amid an "invasion" of Mexicans.

The US Congress responded with the Immigration Reform and Control Act of 1986 (IRCA). Using a two-pronged approach to immigration reform, the IRCA offered to legalize migrants who had been in the country before January 1, 1982, and provided amnesty for those who had worked for at least ninety days in agriculture in the twelve months preceding May 1986. This made it possible for 2.3 million Mexicans in the US to acquire green cards (granting legal status). The second prong of the IRCA involved a major increase in efforts to limit migration to the US. Border security was improved, and the Border Patrol and INS saw significant increases in their enforcement budgets.

The IRCA produced a major shift in the patterns of Mexican migration to the US. It allowed a growing number of Mexicans to settle permanently, and made it possible for these migrants to bring their families across the border. By the early 1990s, 50,000 family members were joining their migrant fathers and partners legally per year, creating a significant shift in the gender and age composition of the migrant population. Legal US residents were less frequently forced into agricultural labor, and created networks in urban areas for recent migrants to move into previously untapped labor markets.

The IRCA did not stop illegal immigration, which continued at around 250,000 per year in the late 1980s, although these migrants found it increasingly difficult to cross the border, and returned home less frequently. Many felt marooned in the US, especially if they had petitions for residency pending and could not leave the country. The easy circulation that characterized earlier eras became less and less common, and after 1990, only about 10 percent of migrants returned home regularly. By the mid-1990s the number of Mexicans living in the US had risen to over 7 million. Two and a half million of these were undocumented (some suggest this number was closer to 5 million).

The IRCA also did little to quell the rising hostility toward Mexicans in the US. Anti-immigrant fervor was particularly strong in California, where about 60 percent of Mexican immigrants settled. In 1994 Pete Wilson was elected governor of California partly on the strength of his endorsement of Proposition 187, a referendum initiative that called for a ban on education, health, and welfare services for illegal immigrants, and required government employees to report those suspected of receiving services (the proposition passed by 59 percent to 41 percent of the vote). California officials were also key proponents of the federal Illegal Immigration Reform and

Immigrant Responsibility Act of 1996, which banned non-citizens from most social services, raised the requirements for sponsoring relatives, and made the deportation of immigrants easier.

These laws further exacerbated the differences between legal and undocumented residents of the US. Legal migrants responded to the 1996 immigration reform by applying for citizenship in record numbers, a practice that offers more opportunities for migration by their family members, and might portend a future in which immigrant Mexicans become a powerful voting bloc. Undocumented migrants, on the other hand, became more vulnerable, and their attempts to migrate more costly.

After 1994 the border itself became a more dangerous place for the undocumented migrant. In the mid-1990s the Border Patrol was increased to 8,200 agents,[4] and its budget was increased from $374 million to $952 million. On October 1, 1994 the Border Patrol launched Operation Gatekeeper, which aimed to disrupt the traditional movement of migrants who crossed between the Pacific Ocean and San Diego's Otay Mesa. The Border Patrol in the area was more than doubled, from 980 to 2,264, and 302 new Border Inspectors were assigned to the area (bringing the total to 504). The old 19-mile fence was replaced by 42.4 miles of primary fencing and 4.8 miles of multi-layer fencing. Other innovations included 6 miles of permanent high-intensity lighting (up from 1 mile), a dramatic expansion in the number of infrared scopes and underground sensors, a new identity system, computers, vehicles, and helicopters.[5] Gatekeeper was followed by similar projects, Operation Hold-the-Line in Texas, and Operation Safeguard in Arizona.

Gatekeeper and its corollaries have entailed a significant militarization of the border, and a concomitant demonization of the Mexican migrant as an invader. It is thus not surprising that members of the Border Patrol have often internalized the xenophobia of American politics, and taken their anger out on the migrants. In recent years migrants have told of an increasing level of abuse suffered at the hands of US officials, which at times has included shootings, beatings, the denial of food, blankets, and medical attention, sexual abuse, and the repeated use of derogatory racial remarks. These abuses continued even after the INS created a Citizens Advisory

Panel in 1994, and was dramatically illustrated when a US Marine on border patrol fatally shot an eighteen-year-old near the Texas frontier in May 1997. The dead youth was a US citizen.

American corporations are now more likely to demand papers from their workers, but are often lax in investigating the authenticity of those papers, as recent scandals at Tyson Foods and Wal-Mart demonstrate. Anti-immigrant legislation has forced Mexican migrants to adopt new strategies, finding new and often more dangerous routes into the country, buying false documents, digging tunnels, paying an ever higher price to the coyotes (as the smugglers of human cargoes are known), but it has not had much effect on the underlying causes of migration. Today there are between 8 and 10 million Mexican migrants in the US.[6] A majority of these Mexicans are legal residents, and about 300,000 more establish permanent residency in the US per year, but between 3 and 5 million of these migrants remain undocumented. About half of these undocumented migrants have lived in the US for ten years or longer, though illegal migrants continue to enter at a rate of nearly 500,000 per year. For them, the violence and injustices they suffer crossing into and working in the US are merely necessary costs borne for the opportunity to earn a living.

In the San Diego area, Operation Gatekeeper has pushed migrants into the Tecate Mountains and deserts to the east of the city, where night-time temperatures in winter routinely fall below freezing. Migrants find it easier to cross in these regions, but have paid a heavy price. In the first five years of the program 444 migrants died along this section of the border. Since 1999 between 300 and 400 migrants have died along this portion of border every year. About eighty of the deaths annually are due to exposure in the mountains, while the rest generally die of exposure in the Imperial Desert or drown in the All American Canal, which separates Calexico and Mexicali.

This tragedy may soon come to an end, though not due to any humanitarian ethos. Fearful that terrorists might potentially use this region to sneak into the US, the federal government is promising to spend billions of dollars extending the fence farther into the mountains. The project promises to destroy the estuary of the Tijuana river, and is opposed by environmentalist groups on both sides of the border, but has been given a green light by the federal government for "national security" reasons.

Lives of the migrants

Mexican migration to the US has historically been characterized by a number of demographic phenomena. The overwhelming majority of migrants are young males, and more than half come from a limited number of states, including Guanajuato, Jalisco, Michoacán, Durango, San Luis Potosí, and Zacatecas. Nowadays they enter a community of Mexicans (both US and Mexican born) that numbers 23 million, constituting one of the largest minority groups in the country. Before the IRCA these migrants sought work primarily in California, Texas, Illinois, Arizona, and New Mexico, but since the 1990s Mexicans have spread throughout the country to meet the needs of US employers. Today Mexicans can be found picking apples in Washington State, working in slaughterhouses in Wisconsin, doing stoop labor in Georgia, and working in some of the fanciest restaurants in New York.

The sheer number of Mexicans living in the US suggests an extremely varied experience. Those born in the country, often to parents and grandparents who were either born there themselves or migrated decades ago, might speak little or no Spanish, have perhaps never even been to Mexico, and qualify for the identity Mexican mostly by virtue of census categories and the celebration of a distinctly US-oriented *mexicanidad*. The holiday that connects many *chicanos* (the term used to describe US citizens of Mexican descent) to their distant origins, Cinco de Mayo, is much more important north of the border than in Mexico.[7] Furthermore, while many *chicanos* remain poor relative to US median incomes, over the generations millions of Mexicans in the US have prospered to such a degree that even poor *chicanos* generally enjoy a standard of living that dwarfs that of their distant relatives in Mexico. Americans of Mexican origin are now business and civic leaders throughout the country, and have been elected or appointed to high offices as both Republicans and Democrats. In 2005 the Republican Alberto González was appointed attorney general of the US, and Antonio Villaraigosa, a Democrat, was elected the first Latino[8] mayor of Los Angeles in more than a century.

Recent migrants are not generally as upwardly mobile, but have nevertheless seen a profound change in their fortunes since migrating to the US. Since the IRCA several million Mexicans have become legal residents of the United States. These immigrants often face discrimination and do not enjoy limitless opportunities, but have much higher standards of living than they could attain in Mexico. Dynamic and hard working, legal residents and their children often identify more closely with American society than Mexican. A growing number own homes, have well-paid jobs, and can reasonably hope to provide college educations and a solidly middle-class future for their children. Migrants working in the meat packing industry in the Midwest have been particularly prosperous, earning a fraction of the wages of the union laborers they replaced, but still enough to substantially improve their standard of living. Like poor migrants from throughout the world, they have had to make enormous sacrifices to achieve this – working multiple jobs, living in cramped housing, and pooling their savings – but those sacrifices have not been in vain for those who have managed to secure a future in the US.

For the undocumented migrants, life in the US is much more difficult. Lacking the papers they need to enter the country legally, they are forced to pay a coyote hundreds (sometimes thousands) of dollars to ferry them across the border. With the increasing presence of the Border Patrol – and now armed militias roaming the border looking for "terrorists" – these migrants may lose all their investment in a coyote if they are picked up and the coyote is identified by US officials. If they cross the border successfully, migrants face further journeys of thousands of miles, to St Louis, Chicago, North Carolina, Georgia, and elsewhere. They rely on the networks set up by their coyotes to move across the country to locales where communities of other migrants (brothers, cousins, and friends) have jobs and living arrangements waiting. While in the US they may sleep twenty to a room (recently in Farmingville, Long Island, police raided a 1,000-square-foot house that was accommodating up to sixty-four migrants. Each migrant paid approximately $225 per month to reside in the house), eat sparingly, and work seemingly endless days in the hope of contributing to the flow of remittances sent to Mexican cities, towns, and villages.

Mostly the migrants are young men, leaving wives, girlfriends, children, and parents at home for months or years at a time. Recently, however, female migration has surged. Some thrive in this environment, working, building new networks, and gradually cutting their ties with their home communities. Others, however, suffer loneliness and depression, and feel deeply isolated in an alien culture and working in a language they do not understand very well. Drugs and alcohol take their toll, and slow deaths in the US or an eventual return to poverty at home become their only options. If they return home, they generally find the same lack of opportunity and sense of desperation that prompted them to migrate in the first place.

Dollars and cents

North American pundits and politicians commonly assume that undocumented migrants act as a drain on the US economy. They calculate the cost of educating the children of undocumented workers, imagine that millions of Mexicans are illegally collecting welfare or undergoing expensive procedures in US hospitals, or lament the high costs of protecting the American border from illegal crossings. There may be some truth to some of these claims, yet the evidence overwhelmingly indicates that Mexican migrants, legal and otherwise, perform essential roles in the US economy. Far from being a drag on the US economy and government, they are critical to American prosperity.

Migrants perform tasks that US citizens refuse to undertake, either because of the wages or the nature of the work. They are the backbone of the agricultural economy, and work in the most arduous sectors of the manufacturing economy. Without migrants the hotel and restaurant industries would need to shut their doors, and those manufacturing industries that remain in the US would be driven overseas. Supermarket prices would jump precipitously, creating a chain reaction of inflation, unemployment, and recession throughout the economy.

Mexican migrants likewise form the core of the domestic service economy, working as nannies, domestic servants, and gardeners throughout the country. Even the government relies on their labor. The US Treasury saves billions of dollars from tax refunds that are never processed because of false social security numbers. Social security counts on $7 billion annually in contributions from illegal immigrants to balance its books, working on the assumption that the illegal migrants cannot collect on the contributions that they make. Nativist politicians ignore these inconvenient facts, preferring to demonize Mexicans with the image of a pregnant migrant leaping the fence so that she can have her baby in an American hospital and raise her child on welfare.

Lacking any political clout, the illegal immigrant is an easy target. Unlike legal residents, they lack the ability to apply for citizenship and join a growing population of Latino voters, a group that both parties now court for support. Moreover, they cannot even depend on legal migrants or Latinos to be universally sympathetic to their plight. In many cases Latinos must compete with undocumented migrants in the labor market, or struggle to distinguish themselves from the illegal migrant in the eyes of their fellow citizens.

Migrants also play a critical role in the economy of their home country. Remittances sent home by Mexicans have grown exponentially in recent years. Remittances totaled $699 million in 1980, but rose to $6.5 billion in 2000. They will likely exceed $20 billion in 2005. Remittances are now the third most important source of foreign revenue (in 2001 oil was $12.8 billion and manufacturing was $141.3 billion). Calculated in terms of balance of trade they are the second most important source of revenue behind only oil and gas (manufacturing has a negative impact, and tourism contributes less than $3 billion).

Most scholars believe that remittances are critical to the survival strategies of as many as a third of rural Mexicans. Some dispute this figure, suggesting that remittances do not overwhelmingly go to poor families, but often include payments for goods imported from Mexico and other financial transactions.[9] That said, even if the dissenters are correct, it seems clear that as government social spending declined in absolute terms in recent years, remittances have acted as a kind of welfare program, allowing communities that might otherwise collapse to survive. In some regions remittances constitute as much as 30 percent of community income, and they pay for more than food. Remittances pay for the construction and upkeep of schools, hospitals, and roads, along with local fiestas.

The sheer volume of remittances has transformed Mexican communities on both sides of the border. Remittances elevate some families while leaving others mired in poverty, creating new impetuses for migration among both the better off (who want to improve their status further) and the poor (who see migration as survival). In parts of Mexico this has had the effect of producing well-appointed ghost towns, replete with beautiful churches, public buildings, and schools paid for by migrants, but with few people to enjoy them.

Through their financial clout migrants sometimes become the most powerful members of their communities even as they live on the other side of the border. Zacatecan politicians, for example, know that they need the support of the migrants to win office, and often troll more effectively for campaign contributions in Los Angeles than at home. Return migrants are also running for office, changing the political landscape in noticeable ways. This trend has accelerated since the mid-1990s, when the Mexican Congress passed a law allowing Mexicans with US citizenship to retain their Mexican citizenship. More change is in store in 2006, when migrants living in the US will gain the right to vote in Mexican elections.

To date, the influence of the migrants has mostly been monetary. In the past decade Zacatecan clubs in the US have raised over $10 million for public works in their state, and are currently working directly with the state government under a program called Three for One, which pledges three pesos of state support for every peso invested in public works by Zacatecans in the US. Implemented nationally by Fox, the program promises critical resources for public works, but it has its critics. Since the migrants choose the projects, the program effectively reallocates public funds into projects favored by individuals who no longer reside in the community. Three for One has already renovated more than a hundred churches.

Fox's moment

Given their growing clout, it is not surprising that President Fox made Mexican migrants a centerpiece of his foreign policy. For several decades PRI presidents did little or nothing to advocate for the interests of undocumented laborers living in the US with their northern neighbors. Violence along the border, prejudicial laws, the routine denial of civil rights, and in the extreme, the refusal of American courts to grant Mexicans in the US charged with serious crimes access to their consulates caused a great deal of anger in Mexico, but PRI governments generally tried to avoid serious confrontations on these issues. Fox, by contrast, imagined Mexico not as a subordinate to the US but as a partner, linked by a common market, and (after 2000) a common commitment to human rights, freedom, and democracy.

Fox could accomplish some of his goals without the aid of the Bush administration. He instructed Mexico's forty-six consulates in the US to extend more support to the migrants, and launched a program that issued more than a million Consular Identification Cards to Mexicans living in the country, to serve as a form of identification in lieu of green cards.[10] The Mexican government convinced thirty-six counties, 119 municipalities, 900 police departments, and 150 banks to accept the cards as identification, allowing undocumented Mexicans to obtain drivers' licenses, leases, and bank accounts. As a result, Mexican immigrants have opened accounts worth $100 million in thirty different Midwestern banks since 2001. Fox also pressed for reforms to ease the transfer of money to Mexico, opening up competition in the market, and reducing the fees by more than 50 percent.

Even so, these reforms could have a limited impact on the lives of migrants without immigration reform in the US. In late 2000 Fox pressed the American president-elect to change US immigration policy. Given the importance of Mexicans to the US economy – a fact tacitly acknowledged by the incoming president, George W. Bush – Fox hoped to leverage a good working relationship with Bush into a reform agenda (during his visit to Texas prior to the inauguration, Bush and Fox called themselves the *"dos amigos"*).[11]

Fox envisioned a solution to the immigrant problem as a type of NAFTA-plus, in which labor would move across the border as freely as goods. As a candidate, Bush seemed open to the idea, especially since the businessmen who supported him saw this as an opportunity to secure a legal, low-wage workforce. When Fox brought up the idea after the election, specifically proposing that the US offer an amnesty or regularization for the millions of undocumented Mexicans in the country, Bush's response was less enthusiastic, though he did not dismiss the idea. He agreed to create a working group, mandated with creating a framework for a migration policy that "ensures humane treatment, legal security, and dignified labor conditions." Meetings began in April 2001, and the group quickly concluded that the reform agenda needed to include regularization of undocumented workers, a guest worker program, increased numbers of visas for Mexican migrants, and economic development in Mexico in order to reduce migration. Mexican officials agreed to meet a number of American concerns by improving border security and restricting the flow of migrants to dangerous parts of the border.

American officials generally favored an approach that advanced only a portion of the agenda. In August 2001, US ambassador to Mexico Jeffrey Davidow suggested that reform begin with a guest worker program. This was the approach favored by most Republicans, who tended to oppose regularization. For obvious reasons the AFL-CIO took the opposite approach, opposing a guest worker program while favoring regularization. For its part, the Mexican government wanted to implement the entire agenda. At first Mexican officials were willing to see it implemented gradually, over four to six years, but when Fox visited Washington in early September, he took a gamble and demanded that all provisions of the working group be agreed to by the end of 2001. Foreign Minister Jorge Castañeda famously summarized this point of view, demanding "the whole enchilada."

It might seem that the terrorist attacks in the US on September 11, 2001 killed the possibility of immigration reform, but even during Fox's visit prior to the attacks, President Bush made it clear that he would not accede to Fox's demands. The Republican majority simply would not agree to a major immigration reform, because while it was popular in the business sector and among some Latinos, the Republican base was so strongly opposed that any major reform of the type envisioned by Fox would have stalled in Congress. Moreover, Fox's demands left many Republicans bristling because they seemed like an unwelcome intrusion into domestic affairs. With the attacks, this contentious issue disappeared into the political abyss.

Two critical changes followed the events of September 2001. First, Americans became increasingly anxious about the insecurity of their borders. Ignoring the fact that the attackers had not entered the US from Canada or Mexico, the public and many commentators took aim at the country's porous borders. Between September and October 2001 the number of Americans who supported greater immigration restrictions rose from 41 to 58 percent. As anxieties about national security rose, the poor, foreign and brown-skinned Mexican morphed into a threat that was perhaps as serious as that posed by Middle Eastern extremists in the eyes of many Americans. This fear was stoked by the musings of national security officials, who predicted that in the future al-Qaeda operatives might slip into the US from Mexico (though there is no evidence that any ever has). These fears begat new anti-immigrant initiatives in Congress and several border states.

Federal officials have further militarized the border under the Department of Homeland Security, increasingly defending their actions as critical to the preservation of American lives. At the state level, voters have increasingly turned against migrants. In 2003, voter rage in California over Governor Gray Davis's decision to sign a bill allowing undocumented migrants to obtain drivers' licenses contributed to his recall. Arnold Schwarzenegger, the new governor, immediately repealed the law.[12] Voters in Arizona passed Proposition 200, which requires residents to show proof of legal status to obtain social services, in 2004. Going farther, the Arizona legislature is currently negotiating to build a private prison in Sonora to house illegal immigrants who have committed crimes in the US. Officials in New Hampshire recently started charging undocumented migrants with criminal trespass on the basis of their unauthorized presence in the United States.[13]

Federal and state officials have also empowered private individuals to fight this version of the War on Terror. In February 2005 the US House of Representatives passed a law that empowered bounty hunters to go after immigrants who have ignored deportation orders. Bush hailed the measure as an important victory in the fight against terrorism, apparently unconcerned that recently a growing number of immigrants have been held at gunpoint by vigilantes. In April 2005 twenty-four-year-old Patrick Haab held seven Mexicans at gunpoint for several hours at an inter-state rest-stop in Arizona, claiming he was making a citizen's arrest of illegal immigrants. The Maricopa County district attorney declined to press charges.

More ominously, in April 2005 a group called the Civil Homeland Defense (CHD) began operating a civilian defense force in the San Pedro River Valley in Arizona. Their "Minuteman Project" (a reference to the militias that played a critical role in the US revolution) includes nearly a thousand volunteers and thirty pilots who patrol the border, armed with no law enforcement expertise whatsoever. Though they insist that they will not confront illegal immigrants, many go about armed and dressed in military fatigues while on patrol. Fox protested against the Minuteman Project, but to little effect, and similar groups are planned for California.[14]

The second critical change that followed the September 11 attacks entailed a new US foreign policy that constructed the world in Manichean terms. Friends and supporters of the US were embraced, while opponents and critics were vilified, if not added to the "axis of evil." Many nations – the cheese-eating French, the terrorist-loving Canadians, and the politically suspect countries of Latin America – were caught in this category, but few were as vulnerable as Mexico. Sensing the changing winds, in the aftermath of the attacks Fox did tighten security on the border. He spoke of Mexico as part of a North American Security Area, increased intelligence-sharing with the US, and detained hundreds of suspected supporters of terrorism. He even went so far as to secretly ask Fidel Castro to avoid a potentially difficult meeting with Bush at a UN summit in Monterrey in 2002, a move that became deeply embarrassing when Castro released an audio tape of the conversation, making Fox seem like a US lackey.[15]

And yet this lackey has found few friends in the US. American papers suggested that Mexican support in the time of crisis was at best lukewarm, and took note that Fox did not visit the States immediately after the attacks to express support. At home, Mexicans turned against both Fox and the US. Fifty-four percent of Mexicans expressed sympathy for the US in October 2001, but by March 2003 a majority of Mexicans were unsympathetic, and almost 30 percent expressed open hostility. Much of this change reflected Mexican responses to unilateral US intervention in the Middle East, but Mexicans also resented the increasingly intransigent US policies in Latin America, particularly vis-à-vis Cuba and Venezuela.

These trends might have gone unnoticed in the US, but for the fact that as part of his efforts to raise Mexico's international profile, Fox sought and won a seat for his country on the UN Security Council for the 2002/03 term. As the Bush administration pressed the Security Council to authorize an invasion of Iraq, he exerted particular pressure on the Mexican representative, Adolfo Aguilar Zinser. In Mexico, however, the cause was so unpopular that Fox feared a complete loss of face if he supported the US, and he refused to authorize the use of force against Iraq. The confrontation prompted a rise in Fox's popularity at home, but Bush fumed, commentators on the Fox News Network vowed that the Mexicans would pay for their crime, and hopes of improving the plight of undocumented Mexicans living in the US seemed more remote than ever.

During 2003 and 2004 numerous angry salvoes were exchanged between the US and Mexico. In January 2003 Jorge Castañeda resigned as minister of foreign relations, blaming failed negotiations with the US over immigration for his decision. Some time later Zinser complained that the US wanted merely a "relationship of convenience and subordination" with Mexico. He resigned his position soon thereafter. In a further blow, in May 2003 Republican representative for North Carolina Cass Ballenger sponsored a non-binding resolution that declared that any agreement with Mexico over migration must include a provision opening up PEMEX to US investment. The Mexican response was predictable.

After a number of very public snubs by Bush, the two presidents began to repair their personal relationship at the Summit of the Americas in Monterrey in 2004. In the US, Bush proposed a minor (and doomed) reform of US immigration policy that would create a limited guest worker program with no promise of permanent residency. Fox hoped to press the issue further at a presidential summit in March 2005, but in spite of his objections Bush insisted in Congress that Canadian prime minister Paul Martin be included.

This ensured that the US agenda would dominate; migration issues were marginalized.

Even as Fox and Bush repaired their personal relationship, official sniping at Mexico has continued, even escalated. In spite of all Mexican efforts to cooperate, the US State Department continues to complain openly about drug smuggling, corruption, migration, and the potential terrorist threat along the border, describing the border region as an area of high insecurity for the US. In December 2004 Mexico's Ministry of Foreign Relations threw more fuel on the fire by publishing 1.5 million copies of a pamphlet called the *Guide for the Mexican Migrant*. The thirty-one-page guide was designed to decrease the dangers of migration, and reduce potential conflicts and problems with immigration officials for those caught. The pamphlet also provided advice that would help migrants avoid detection. Three hundred Mexicans lost their lives trying to enter the US in 2004, and Mexicans generally welcomed the information provided. US officials described it as a how-to manual for law-breakers.

What terrifies Mexicans

Since 2001 it has been obvious that Americans are afraid. They fear Islamic militants, they feared Saddam Hussein, and many fear homosexuality, liberal values, and a decline in Christianity in American life. Many also fear immigrants, and believe that immigrants bring crime, lax morality, and drugs into their country. These fears have coalesced in President Bush's War on Terror.

Mexicans do not share all these fears; in fact a majority of Mexicans seem to be indifferent or hostile to Bush's War on Terror, especially inasmuch as it has impacted on the lives of their compatriots negatively. And yet Mexico has been undergoing its own war on terror in recent times, a struggle that centers on another kind of border crossing, the largely unrestrained flow of illicit drugs into the US from Mexico. As with Bush's war, the results of Mexican efforts to stem the flow of drugs do not seem to have made the country a safer place. Rather, they have made Mexico a more frightened, and in some cases more frightening, place.

Fox has made a number of specific efforts to promote the security and safety of Mexicans. In 2001 he created a new Office of Human

Rights. He also created a Ministry of Public Security, and profession-alized and expanded the Federal Preventative Police (PFP), an agency founded by Zedillo in 1999. Continuing a long-term trend toward militarizing domestic security, he appointed General Rafael Macedo de la Concha as attorney general, and created a new national police force called the Federal Agency of Investigations (AFI), which was modeled on the FBI, and drew heavily from military personnel. Fox also reformed the office of attorney general to give greater autonomy to prosecutors in going after the drug traffickers.

These reforms have produced some spectacular successes. In early 2002 Ramón Arellano Félix was killed in a shoot-out with local police in Mazatlán, and Benjamin Arellano Félix was arrested in the state of Puebla. Osiel Cárdenas, alleged leader of the Gulf cartel, was arrested in March 2003. In smaller operations dozens of police officers and customs officials suspected of corruption were fired, and some arrested. These arrests were accompanied by a number of seizures, including the confiscation of 7 tons of marijuana in Nuevo Laredo, Tamaulipas, in January 2004. In January 2005 Juan José Álvarez Tostado, leader of the Juárez drug cartel previously run by Amado Carrillo Fuentes, was arrested in Mexico City, and Augustín Vásquez-Mendoza, wanted in the US for killing a DEA agent, was extradited to the States.

And yet these spectacular successes were accompanied by even more spectacular acts of violence that reverberated throughout Mexico. Kidnappings in Mexico now average around three thousand per year. A wave of murders in Chihuahua has left several hundred women dead and captured the nation's attention (see Chapter 7). Today there is more violence against journalists in Mexico than in any other country in the Americas. Mexico lagged behind only Iraq, Bangladesh, and the Philippines in the number of journalists killed during 2004. In one of the more spectacular cases, Raúl Gibb Guerrero, the editor and publisher of *La Opinión*, in the town of Poza Rica, Veracruz, was ambushed in his car on a Veracruz highway and shot repeatedly after his paper published stories about drug traf-ficking and gasoline theft in the region. Other editors murdered in 2004 included Roberto Javier Mora García, editor of *El Mañana* in Nuevo Laredo, Tamaulipas, and Leodegario Aguilera Lucas, editor of *Mundo Político* in Acapulco. No one has been convicted of any of the crimes, and lately the attacks have taken an even bolder tone. In early 2005 the daughter of journalist Cecilia Vargas was kidnapped, held for several hours, and beaten.

On Tuesday, June 22, 2004, Francisco Ortiz Franco, reporter and editor at *Zeta*, was executed in front of his two small children. *Zeta* speculated that the killing was ordered by Jorge Hank Rhon, candidate for Tijuana mayor. A week later 250,000 people participated in one of the largest demonstrations Mexico City has ever seen. Clad mostly in white, marchers came from fourteen different states to demand that the government take some action against the perpetrators of violence in Mexico. Many carried pictures of family members and friends who had been victims. Others carried placards demanding the death penalty for kidnappers and condemning a corrupt and ineffective judiciary.

Counter-demonstrators heckled the crowd. Carrying banners that equated crime and violence in Mexico with neo-liberalism, they pointed to the large numbers of middle-class marchers as a sign that this protest did not reflect the concerns of most Mexicans. Poor Mexicans, they claimed, saw nothing new in the violence of Mexican cities. To be sure, some of the protesters betrayed their class credentials when they ended the march with a visit to a nice café or museum, and rode the subway for the first time in years on their way home, or simply waited for the crowds to disperse so they could hail a taxi. Some had become wealthier as other Mexicans had grown poorer, and the homes they returned to were in gated communities, where their bodyguards and armored cars protected them from the worst of the violence. Yet crime affects more than just the middle class. Crime and violence in recent years has affected Mexicans of all social classes, and have expanded beyond the borders and slums of Mexico City to all parts of the country. Thousands of marchers on that day were from less prosperous sectors of society, and violence against poor people was on many minds. More than this, though larger social and economic changes did not seem to be a goal of many demonstrators, the cross-class protesters shared a common loathing for the judicial system in Mexico. Eschewing the slogans of the various political parties, their claim was that the apparatuses of the Mexican state had collapsed, and that safety could come only once those structures were remade.

The explicit connection between the illegal drug trade and the violence was not lost on most marchers, and has only been made more evident since June 2004. In the first half of 2005 around eight hundred Mexicans died in drug-related violence, and a growing number of these victims have been members of the agencies created to fight the traffickers.[16] Much of the recent violence can be traced to Joaquín Guzmán Loera, who escaped from a prison near Guadalajara in a laundry truck in January 2001 and rebuilt his organization by attacking the Gulf cartel and the Arellano Félix brothers. His enemies have recruited ex-special-forces personnel, known as the Zetas, and directed a war from inside La Palma prison, where Osiel Cárdenas, working with Benjamin Arellano Félix, has battled to retain his share of the trade. Massacres of five of Guzmán's associates in Nuevo Laredo in October 2004 were followed by the murder of nine Cárdenas associates (including three federal agents, tortured, bound, shot in the head, and dumped next to an airport) in Cancún in November.

On December 31, 2004, Guzmán's brother Arturo was shot several times at close range in the visiting area at La Palma prison. The resulting investigation implicated several prison officials, and revealed serious problems at the jail. Investigators found that at least nine trucks with supplies were entering La Palma every day, far in excess of the allowed limit, and searches of the prison found electronic appliances, cell phones, drugs, and large quantities of food. When 148 workers at the prison were given polygraph tests, less than one-third passed. Seeing these results, Fox ordered a prison takeover by 750 troops and police in mid-January 2005. A week later six prison guards were found dead in an SUV within sight of the maximum-security prison in Matamoros, presumably killed in revenge for the takeover at La Palma. Federal officials responded by taking over Matamoros.

That federal officials seem unable to control their maximum-security prisons is alarming to Mexicans, but not nearly as frightening as the recent spate of violence in border cities. Perhaps the worst affected has been Nuevo Laredo, a city of 300,000 on the Tamaulipas frontier with the US. For some time this city has been the site of a turf war between the Sinaloa and Gulf cartels. By official counts sixty-eight people were killed in Nuevo Laredo in 2004 (unofficial estimates are more than twice that), and another sixty-nine died in the first half of 2005. Since 2000 sixty-two police officers, including eleven AFI agents, have been killed here. Many of the killings can be attributed to the Zetas, who control much of the city, and have recently shown a taste for the types of public executions that tend to take the lives of bystanders. May and June 2005 were particularly violent, punctuated by the murder of two police chiefs. On June 1, police chief Enrique Cárdenas was murdered at his home as he prepared to take his daughter to school. His replacement, Alejandro Domínguez Coello, was killed six hours after being named police chief on June 8. Just days before the second murder, forty-one local police officers opened fire on twenty-five AFI agents who had been assigned to the city to help them fight the drug traffickers.

With the attack on the AFI agents, Fox had seen enough. On June 12 he launched Operation Secure Mexico, a coordinated effort between 1,000 agents of the army, AFI, and PFP to impose the rule of law in Baja California, Sonora, and Tamaulipas, along with select parts of the Federal District and Mexico State. When the military arrived in the Nuevo Laredo, they sequestered the police in their barracks, disarmed them, and forced them to submit to drug and polygraph tests, along with background checks. One hundred and fifty police in Nuevo Laredo were arrested. Of the 725 local police investigated, only 290 were cleared of wrongdoing.

The National Commission on Human Rights condemned Secure Mexico, calling it a violation of the human rights of the police. Opponents made their anger public when on Friday, June 17, an organization that claimed to represent the families of the detained police officers held a rally in Nuevo Laredo, demanding the departure of the AFI and PFP, and the return of the city to local control. They angrily denounced the *"chilangos"*[17] who had taken over their city, and at one point grew so animated that they tried to force their way into Mayor Daniel Peña Treviño's office. Police eventually dispersed the crowd.

A little while later, the surreal quality of contemporary life in

Nuevo Laredo again surfaced. At about 4:30 in the afternoon, long after the protest had broken up, two men "who looked like *cholos*" approached a green Chevy Blazer with Texas license plates that was parked in front of the mayor's office, and opened fire with a 40-caliber revolver. Moments later a man named Filoberto Peña Berlanga lay dead in his car, and his mother and three-year-old son were bleeding from gunshot wounds. Reporters in Laredo, on the US side of the border, quickly added Peña to the list of the dozens of Americans who have been kidnapped or killed while visiting Nuevo Laredo in recent times. His father told reporters that Peña, a former Nuevo Laredo police officer, had simply been in town for a visit, and was the unfortunate victim of circumstance. The local AFI and PFP immediately designated his death a drug-related shooting, part of an ongoing cycle of retribution among traffickers. They did not even preserve the scene, ensuring that there would be no evidence gathered by investigators.

As the details of Peña's recent activities came to light, however, the circumstances surrounding his death became even murkier. When journalists studied photos taken earlier in the day at the protest, they repeatedly came across photos of Peña. It turned out that Peña had been one of the most vocal leaders of the demonstration, openly challenging federal agents, and had in fact been the individual who called for protesters to lynch the mayor, at one point personally trying to force his way into the municipal offices. Reporters also started to look more closely at the protest, concluding that although it had been organized in support of the local police, very few families of local police officers seemed to be in attendance. *La Jornada* described the rally as follows: "Necklaces, bracelets, and large gold medallions were *de rigueur* among the organizers, who rented several trucks to transport the protestors, who were in turn offered food, water, music, and even new parasols to protect them from the sun." It turned out that many of the people at the protest were directly involved in the local drug trade, mostly as street-level drug dealers making their living selling to foreign tourists.

Reporters were particularly perplexed that the two men who fired the shots were not apprehended, in spite of the overwhelming presence of police in the area, and the fact that the assassination took place just meters away from the local police headquarters. The implications of these facts are fairly clear. For whatever reason, Filoberto Peña's killers knew they could execute him in broad daylight, in the middle of Nuevo Laredo, without any risk to themselves. That this type of lawlessness can exist at the heart of their cities is something that terrifies Mexicans.

Locals are also uneasy about the militarization of the city, but many find this alternative preferable to living in constant fear of the traffickers, and hope that Secure Mexico might help establish the rule of law in the long run. As in other parts of the country, people in the region have long demanded a substantive response to an out-of-control situation.[18] News that federal agents had rescued forty-three kidnapped people from two houses thus sent waves of hope and excitement through the community on June 26. Many of those rescued appeared to have been tortured, and told of being kidnapped by local police and turned over to the Zetas. Some had been detained for several months.

No one could reasonably argue that the release of these kidnap victims was not as much a moral imperative as the defense of the civil liberties of Nuevo Laredo's policemen. If Secure Mexico produces greater public safety in the border region, even at the expense of human rights and transparent government, a significant number of people in the region (except, of course, those who benefit from the illegal drug trade) will feel that it was well worth the sacrifice. On the other hand, if the militarization of policing along the border simply leads to more violence, Secure Mexico will seem like just another government farce in a long failed drug war. This is what is at stake in Mexico's war on terror.

6 | A decade of NAFTA

On September 28, 2004 readers of the *New York Times* were treated to a rich assessment of the impact of NAFTA in Mexico. In an article filled with tales of official corruption, the desecration of ancient cultures, and a pastoral rendering of the loss of the family business, readers learned the story of a Wal-Mart that was being built among the ruins of Teotihuacán, an ancient city famous for its pyramids just northeast of Mexico City. True, the store was not actually being built among the ruins, but in the adjacent town, but readers were warned that undisturbed artifacts were likely being destroyed by the construction, and were treated to a photo that showed the store rising directly in the shadow of the Temple of the Moon.

The story was not unusual for the *Times*, whose reporting on Mexico tends to focus on a juxtaposition of the exotic and the Americanized, and which often uses these stories to reflect on the process of North American integration. In this case, the article noted that the new 71,902-square-foot store would destroy some of the local charm and local merchants, but would provide residents of the region with access to much-desired consumer goods, at lower costs and of higher quality than they could then find. The store would also generate 200 jobs and raise wage levels in Teotihuacán. Readers also learned that Wal-Mart had probably bribed local officials to get permission to build the store, and that locals were shut out of the approval process, which involved not a single public hearing.

This was not the first time that *Times* readers had been treated to stories about Wal-Mart in Mexico. Echoing fears north of the border, the paper has from time to time informed readers that Wal-Mart owns 650 stores, supermarkets, and restaurants in Mexico. With annual revenues of $11 billion, Wal-Mart is larger than the three next largest retailers in Mexico combined. Even as a few hundred people protested against the store in Teotihuacán, Mexicans by the millions were shopping in Wal-Mart, helping to boost the company's Mexican profits by nearly 30 percent in the first quarter of 2005. Whether this is a good thing, a bad thing, or neither depends on your politics. At the very least, it is a big thing, and has been one of a number of major transformations that Mexico has undergone since the NAFTA came into effect in 1994.

The new Mexican economy

When Mexico's economy sank into crisis in late 1994, some critics blamed NAFTA, and predicted serious problems for the treaty. They were proved wrong when the economy began emerging from the crisis in late 1995, buoyed by a series of austerity measures implemented by President Zedillo and a rescue package of loans from the US.[1] In 1996 the government pledged a balanced budget, another 5 percent reduction in spending, and more increases in prices for services. As a result of these initiatives, the government moved from a public sector deficit of 1.7 billion pesos in 1994 to an 815 million peso surplus in 1995.

The 1994 crisis turned out to be a crisis in liquidity rather than a sign of fundamental flaws in the economy, particularly vis-à-vis the deficit. The fiscal deficit, a critical cause of the 1982 crisis, was under control in 1994. Foreign lenders returned to Mexico within seven months of the crisis (compared to seven years after 1982), prompting a quick return to growth. After shrinking by 6.2 percent in 1995, GDP grew by 5.1 percent in 1996, and reached its pre-crisis levels by the end of 1996. In the following four years, the rates of growth were 6.8, 4.8, 3.4, and 6.9 percent. Foreign reserves grew to $17.6 billion by end of 1996, and now stand at over 50 billion. Foreign debt, which had risen to $165.6 billion in 1995, shrank to $88.3 billion in 1997. Foreign direct investment also returned to Mexico quickly, and has grown steadily since the late 1990s. Inflation, a critical measure of economic stability, today averages only about 3 percent per year.

The rapid recovery was in part explained by Zedillo's willingness to embrace global trade in response to the crisis. After 1982 the country was paralyzed for almost seven years, a situation made worse by the encumbrances that tariffs, import licenses, and regulations placed on the economy. In 1994 an entirely different regulatory structure was in place, and though the economy was devastated, certain sectors could rapidly take advantage of access to international capital and export markets to repair their businesses. US officials were also quick to put together the $52 billion bail-out in 1995, given fears that a general crisis in the Mexican economy could spill over into the US.

The crisis thus proved to be a relatively brief bump in Mexico's economic transformation during the 1990s. Mexican exports rose from $29.2 billion in 1990 to $189 billion in 2004, making Mexico one of the most important trading nations in the world.[2] And the composition of this trade was transformed dramatically. By the late 1990s manufactured goods made up almost 90 percent of Mexico's sales abroad, while petroleum fell from 20 percent in the early 1990s to 7 percent by the end of the decade. In 1980 the top ten exports were mostly primary goods, but twenty years later only two of the top ten were primary goods.[3]

Between August 1995 and August 1999 one-half of all Mexican jobs created (1 million) were related to the export sector, and workers in these firms generally earned more than those in non-export firms. The *maquila* sector, which increased in size twenty-five times between 1982 and 2001, now accounts for almost half of manufactured exports, and for much of the past decade has been Mexico's second most important source of foreign revenue earnings. In 2001 1.31 million people worked in 3,713 *maquilas*. In 2002 these plants exported about $78 billion worth of goods. *Maquilas* have also expanded beyond the border region. Center-north states have been the most economically dynamic, but manufacturing has grown elsewhere as plant owners have moved to regions where they can pay lower wages. Today a third of national manufacturing takes place in Mexico State and the Federal District. Ownership of the factories is fairly evenly divided between North Americans and Mexicans, a factor that has contributed to a fairly significant expansion in Mexico's bourgeoisie in regions where the plants have been built.

Two (or more) Mexicos

There are more rich people in Mexico today than in 1994; 85,000 Mexicans now have fortunes worth more than $1 million. NAFTA and privatizations have also launched some Mexicans into the strato-sphere of global wealth. The most commonly cited beneficiary is Carlos Slim Helú, who entered the ranks of the super-rich after he acquired Telmex. His conglomerate now controls Telmex, Grupo Carso, US Commercial Corp, América Móvil, Grupo Sanborns, Grupo Financiero Inburso, and others. According to *Forbes* magazine, his assets now exceed $23.8 billion (2005 figure), making him one of the ten richest men in the world, and the first Latin American to join that select group. His fortune represents the equivalent of 43 percent of the annual income of all Mexicans, 24.65 million households. As these figures no doubt suggest, Mexico has one of the most unequal distributions of income in the Americas.[4]

Today 5.4 percent of the nation's wealth is in the hands of eleven individuals, whose combined wealth is $35.5 billion, and continues to grow at a breathtaking rate. Roberto Hernández, with a fortune of $2 billion, made much of his money during the bank reprivatiza-tions. He and Alfredo Harp Helú purchased the Banco Nacional de México, which in 2001 they sold to Citigroup. Other members of this select group include Ricardo Salinas Pliego, who controls Televisión Azteca (which was privatized in 1993), Banco Azteca, and Electra, and Emilio Azcárraga Jean, president of Televisa. Televisa is now the world's largest Spanish-language media company, and its *telenovelas* dominate the genre in Latin America and the United States. Televisa owns a stake in the US network Univisión, and controls TV networks, radio stations, and magazines across Latin America.

Unlike in the past, under NAFTA a growing number of business-men hold their wealth in public companies. This phenomenon is linked to the growing tendency of wealth to be linked to trans-national businesses and the increased role of foreign direct invest-ment in the country, and has created problems for some of Mexico's secretive super-rich. This emerging practice landed Ricardo Salinas Pliego in deep trouble with the US Securities and Exchange Com-mission (SEC) in 2005.[5] Tax avoidance and fraud remain common, often aided by the complicity of public officials, who themselves have historically kept their dealings out of the public eye.

Mexico's high-level public officials have also struggled with the increased transparency of Mexican society, often endeavoring to obscure their salaries in spite of Mexico's recent Freedom of Information Law. They may have good reason to do so. Mexico's president, for example, earns a base salary of 158,027.66 pesos monthly after taxes, but some estimate that with perks and hidden income his compensation is closer to 3 million pesos. Members of the Chamber of Deputies earn a base salary of 122,565 pesos monthly, with perks too numerous to calculate. The salary of the eleven justices of Mexico's Supreme Court is easily calculated, but it exceeds 72 million pesos per year, a figure that *La Jornada* noted would pay 4,428 workers the minimum wage. The president of the court earns 649,433.41 pesos per month, or 7,793,200.96 pesos per year. The other ten justices receive monthly salaries of 793,200.35 pesos. When they retire, their pensions pay them a full salary.[6]

Some of this prosperity seems to have spilled over into other sectors of society. The *maquila* sector, for instance, is no longer characterized by the low-wage, largely female workforce of the past, and now has an almost equal ratio of males to females. Wages in the *maquila* sector now compare favorably to other industrial wages, having grown at a higher rate than wages in domestic manufacturing during the 1990s. Together, these developments underpin an important and ongoing revolution in Mexican gender roles. Today nearly 40 percent of women are active in the workforce (compared to 17.6 percent in 1970). Twenty percent of employed women work in industry. When combined with the 23 percent of women in the business sector, the number of women working in business or industry equals the number of women working in the service sector (traditionally the dominant form of female employment).[7] In spite of the variety of forms of discrimination they face (they may be fired for getting pregnant, face regular harassment, and typically earn less than their male counterparts), paid labor has given women access to more resources and extended social networks, along with new opportunities for political activism, economic independence, and education.[8]

For industrial workers more generally, these changes have not seemed propitious. Workers in the manufacturing sector generally now earn about 75 percent of what they did in 1980, and since 1994 real wages have fallen even in those industries where productivity and profitability have improved. In the automotive sector real wages have fallen over 20 percent even as productivity has risen by more than 60 percent. Labor was particularly weakened when Zedillo did not renew the National Agreement to Increase Productivity and Quality in 1995. Under the terms of the old agreement unions agreed to tie wage increases to productivity increases; this practice ended once the agreement expired. Arguing that any wage increases would undermine competitiveness, most firms negotiated agreements with the CTM and CT that depressed wages. Going farther, in October 1995, as a part of the new Alliance for Economic Recuperation, the unions agreed to fixed rates for price and wage increases that keep wage increases below the rate of inflation. Anger among the rank and file has spurred the growth of alternative unions, including the National Union of Workers (UNT, founded in 1998), but these unions have also had little success in pressing wage demands.

These developments remind us that while export-oriented Mexican conglomerates with access to international markets have prospered since 1994, those Mexicans without access to international markets have faced much dimmer prospects. This contrast is most clearly seen in the agricultural sector. Agricultural exports have bolstered the fortunes of commercial farmers since the early 1990s. Others have been staggered by a doubling of agricultural imports from the US, which has resulted in a significant growth in rural unemployment, declining wages, and migration. Agriculture employed 44 percent of working Mexicans in 1970. Today it employs less than 30 percent.

Today there are 4.5 million units of agricultural production in Mexico.[9] About ten thousand agriculturalists possess lands that average between 1,500 and 7,000 hectares. Almost 3.5 million producers work holdings that average less than 11 hectares; 1.3 million producers in the latter category possess lands averaging just over 1 hectare. In all, the 15,000 largest producers generate half the income produced by Mexican agriculture, and prosper largely owing to their ability to grow fruits, vegetables, and a series of other commodities for the US market. For most of the rest of Mexican farmers, staple producers who sell to the domestic market, the imports of grains, maize, and soybeans under NAFTA have had catastrophic results.

The Mexican government could have protected maize producers for fifteen years under NAFTA, but instead opened the country to unlimited imports almost immediately, making massive purchases of maize in the US even in 1994. Imports of maize now amount to 5–6 million tons per year. Grain imports from the US have increased by more than 70 percent since 1994. After January 1, 2003 all agricultural products from the US and Canada enter Mexico duty free.

The agricultural goods that enter Mexico have already been heavily subsidized by the US and Canadian governments. They compete with Mexican maize and grain which have been produced with almost no government aid. In fact, the government curtailed public investment, price supports, and subsidies even as it opened Mexican agriculture to subsidized foreign competition. This has particularly devastated the 2.5 million peasants who produce 75 percent of Mexico's maize, and promises to devastate other agricultural sectors where the government is forcing producers to compete in the international market. The 440,000 Mexicans who work in sugar-related industries have lost most of their subsidies and face government demands that they modernize and eliminate corruption in the mills in anticipation of a complete elimination of sugar tariffs in 2008. There is little chance that Mexican sugar producers will be able to compete against subsidized US sugar or cheap Caribbean imports.

While agricultural credits have been plentiful for exporters, it remains difficult for domestic producers to access seed, fertilizer, credit, and irrigation. Commercial banks have little interest in peasant agriculture, and the Banco de Crédito Rural (Banrural) was eliminated in 2003 amid huge losses and an astronomical default rate (prior to the 1990s defaults were understood as a type of subsidy). It has also become more difficult for growers to market their products, as there are few buyers and they tend to offer very low prices. Peasants have few supply and distribution mechanisms, making moneylenders and intermediaries extremely powerful. No efforts have been made to create micro-credit and locally oriented development programs, in spite of their successes elsewhere.

In 2002 the government announced a program to protect peasants that it called an Agricultural Shield, but the $10 billion allocated to the program came mainly from monies already committed to agriculture, and the specific agency charged with rural development actually faced budget cuts. After protests the budget for agriculture was increased by 10 percent, but the money came with the threat that subsidies were on their way out; that rural farmers needed to use the money to become competitive or get out of agriculture. For the 50 percent of rural dwellers who have not been participants in the export boom, this is troubling advice. It reminds them of the essential logic of contemporary life; there are now two Mexicos, the Mexico of the peso and the Mexico of the dollar. Those who have been able to take advantage of increases in trade and access to the dollar economy have prospered, but those who traditionally made their incomes from the domestic economy are, according to a popular saying, *jodidos* (the screwed).

Rural maize producers are not just losing a livelihood. Maize cultivation forms a critical part of the cultural fabric of rural Mexico, and lies at the heart of community relations throughout much of the countryside. This is particularly true for indigenous Mexicans, but is also true for millions of mestizo peasants. Maize, it is said, is in the "blood" of Mexican peasants, and its loss would resonate far beyond the rural economy. Moreover, if maize cultivation declines, the world will lose some of the rich biodiversity that small-scale peasant agriculture has created in Mexican maize; a diversity that in the past has provided critical solutions to blight in more prosperous regions. It was maize from Mexico which saved North American maize from the corn leaf blight in 1970.

Those farmers who once saved North American maize are now planting genetically modified (GM) maize in their fields, in spite of a law banning the cultivation of such maize in Mexico. Whether these plantings have been accidental or on purpose, the sheer volume of GM maize coming in from the US has made it impossible to prevent its spread into Mexican fields. Peasants face immediate problems because this maize is designed to regenerate poorly, and cannot be effectively saved for replanting from one season to the next. As consumers they face other problems. Recently several Mexican newspapers and websites across the region have buzzed with the claim that in scientific experiments rats fed GM maize experienced changes in their liver functions and blood chemistry.[10] The findings have been disputed, but suggest that those Mexicans who still make maize a critical part of their diet may have something to fear.

Poverty

For the most part, unionized workers have staved off poverty by relying on the multiple minimum wages they earn, on the labor power of family members, and by taking advantage of the reduced benefits offered by the IMSS, ISSSTE, and SEP. If they are very lucky, they can also count on the fact that they belong to one of the unions that the government continues to protect as a part of its governing strategy (i.e. the PEMEX workers' union). Newer workers might also be able to benefit from the private pension accounts that the government created in 1997, though the overheads in this system and the dangers of market fluctuations may cause their savings to evaporate.[11] Owing to these strategies, in several regions of Mexico working-class people have actually seen improvements in a number of critical areas of quality of life over the past two decades. Their life expectancy is longer, they suffer a lower rate of infant mortality, literacy rates are higher, working Mexicans are spending more years in school, and they are going on to secondary education at a rate that has never been seen before.

Today the IMSS and ISSSTE provide benefits for about 55 percent of Mexicans, and another 33 million have private savings accounts. That said, most new workers, especially those in the informal sector, have no coverage from either the IMSS or ISSSTE, and no chance of accumulating private pensions. These developments are also reflected in long-term changes in the character of poverty in Mexico. There are any number of measures of poverty, but generally it seems that the number of Mexicans living in poverty gradually decreased between 1940 and 1981, when the poverty rate was somewhere between 25 and 50 percent.[12] Poverty rates expanded significantly from 1981 to 1989, gradually decreased until 1995, and then jumped again. Poverty rates have remained relatively stable at between 43 and 51 percent for the past decade, but during the 1990s the number of Mexicans living in extreme poverty rose significantly, from about 16.1 percent in 1992 to 28 percent in 1999. Nearly 80 percent of rural families are poor.

These rural families are not unionized workers with benefits, but form a segment of the population that earns the minimum wage or less. The IMSS estimates that 783,000 workers currently earn the minimum wage (currently 45 pesos per day), while 1.4 million workers earn less than 45 pesos daily. These workers face a minimum wage that is worth about 30 percent of what it was in 1980, and which today pays for barely more than half of the bread basket for a family of five.

The human costs of rural poverty are profound. More than 40 million Mexicans suffer from malnutrition, 7 million suffer from respiratory ailments, 2 million have dysentery, and 10 million lack access to medical care. Infant mortality rates have been falling since the 1960s, but still remain a very high 28 per 1,000 live births. The trend is also regionalized. Social indicators in parts of Chiapas and Oaxaca are among the poorest in the Americas, whereas in northern states like Nuevo Leon they resemble those of some European countries. In Chiapas rates of mortality from infectious disease are three times the national average. Infant mortality in the five poorest states is double that of the five most wealthy states.

Children are often the worst victims of poverty. According to a recent UNICEF study, 28 percent of Mexican children live in poverty, 1.4 million children under five suffer from malnutrition, and almost 30 percent of children suffer from anemia. The most malnourished tend to be rural indigenous children. In many cases government aid has done little to help these people. One newspaper recently reported that poor families in Oaxaca, Puebla, Hidalgo, and Veracruz give baby food distributed by the government to their animals, because their children will not eat it. Neither will many of these children obtain the benefits of an education. UNICEF estimates that 2 million Mexican children of school age never attend school, and that one in three children do not complete nine years of schooling.

Somewhere around 15 percent of school-age children are working instead of attending school. Child labor is especially common in rural areas, but children do factory labor, and work as street vendors and entertainers. These children sometimes work as parts of large family networks, but recent economic dislocations have forced tens of thousands of children to live on the streets, turning to drugs and prostitution to survive (some estimates place the number of children in the sex trade at close to 20,000). They even migrate to the US, at a rate of nearly 150,000 per year.

Salinas, Zedillo, and Fox shared a relatively common approach to poverty, favoring targeted programs over the universal approach that characterized the years prior to 1981. PRONASOL, PROGRESA, and Oportunidades (their respective programs) each sought to identify specific causes of poverty and specific communities where federal monies could be spent most effectively. PROGRESA, for example, was narrowly targeted at health, education, and nutrition, while a variety of food and other subsidies were eliminated.[13] By 2000 2.6 million families were participants in PROGRESA, earning cash in return for the promise that their children would be sent to school, and gaining access to health clinics and pre- and post-natal care. The monies they received, averaging $25 per month, equaled 22 percent of their income.

Oportunidades expanded these efforts, and now operates in every municipality in the country. Even so, fewer than 20 percent of Mexicans receive benefits from the program, and critics argue that programs that endeavor to target poverty – as opposed to general social welfare programs – are inappropriate when at least half and maybe three-quarters of the population live below the poverty line. Critics also note that their tendency to ration benefits makes such programs easily politicized. PRONASOL was used in nakedly political ways, and women beneficiaries of PROGRESA were forced to pledge loyalty to the government in return for their benefits. Fox claims that these abuses have been eliminated within Oportunidades.

Oportunidades promises to turn poor Mexicans into entrepreneurs, individuals who possess capital and have the capacity to be players in the market. Along with health and educational initiatives, Fox has actually tried to offer working-class Mexicans the chance to accumulate the wealth that they need to enter the middle class. One program promises to offer 750,000 mortgages to people earning around $1,000 per month by 2006, allowing them to avoid the traditionally onerous demands of Mexican lenders (high interest rates and a 40 percent down payment) and buy homes valued at $25,000. There is a risk, however. Poor people who become homeowners are only as secure as their next paycheck, or until their already high mortgage rates rise (rates are currently set at 21 percent). Even if all goes well for the mortgage program, and economic stability is maintained, the program will barely meet the demands for new housing, let alone the long-pent-up demand of the more than four million families living in squatter communities that ring the capital. The only assured beneficiaries are the large conglomerates building the houses.

The Fox administration claims that the statistics on poverty in Mexico are improving. Since 2001 the number of people living in extreme poverty has fallen from 24 million to 17 million, a figure that administration officials claim is a sure sign that Oportunidades is working. Others point to rising oil prices and remittances (which are now around $20 billion annually) as the critical reasons why extreme poverty has declined, and claim that these two sources of income hardly amount to an effective economic and social policy.

The beleaguered middle class

Living between the extremes of wealth and poverty, middle-class Mexicans have faced their own sets of pressures and opportunities since NAFTA came into effect in 1994. They have been particularly vulnerable to violence, unable to sequester themselves behind closed gates and hire bodyguards. Taxi kidnappings have been particularly dangerous for the middle class. More significantly, the middle class has generally been unable to secure its wealth abroad, and suffered disproportionately during the peso devaluation in 1994. Those who borrowed money to build businesses or purchase new homes during salinastroika found that while the government protected and promoted the powerful, they were more vulnerable to ruin than ever before.

One of the first significant signs of these vulnerabilities came with the emergence in 1992 of El Barzón, a movement of debt-ridden mid-sized Chihuahuan farmers. Middle class by definition (poor Mexicans rarely even have bank accounts, let alone collateral for loans), the movement represented a dramatic break from traditional middle-class complaisance. They chose a tractor as their symbol, and drew their name from a popular figure from a revolutionary *corrido*[14] about a man who is unable to pay his debt to a *hacendado*. Like the Zapatistas, El Barzón identified with the popular origins of the Mexican Revolution, claiming that as hard-working, honest people, they were its descendants. In fact, given the petit-bourgeois origins of many 1910 revolutionaries, their claim to the revolution was as legitimate as was the EZLN's.

El Barzón rapidly spread, finding adherents among the owners of highly capitalized, modern farming operations who were enraged at a series of illegal practices that Mexican banks were using to foreclose on their operations. Beyond this, members of the movement argued that the banks were making repayment impossible by confiscating equipment they needed to be productive. They demanded both a halt to foreclosures and government help in restructuring loans.

They grew to a national protest movement in 1993, gaining notoriety when members briefly occupied government offices in Autlán, Jalisco. Their growth shadowed a growing crisis of liquidity among middle-class Mexicans. In 1990 just 2.1 percent of loans in the country were overdue, but by 1994, even before the crisis, the percentage of overdue loans had risen to 10.6 percent. Middle-class debtors were devastated by the peso crisis in December 1994, and by October 1996 almost half of all loans were overdue and in danger of default. By this time support for El Barzón had skyrocketed among shopkeepers and middle-class businessmen, making it one of the largest middle-class opposition movements Mexico had even seen.

As the movement grew, supporters took a multi-pronged approach to alleviating middle-class debt. They pressed state legislatures and Congress for bank reforms that would protect them from predatory lending practices. In some states they successfully lobbied for laws that placed moratoriums on auctions of their properties. More generally, El Barzón worked to undermine legislative proposals inimical to their interests. Outside of the legislatures, members of El Barzón filed lawsuits over illegal practices, particularly the practice of compounding interest by adding it to the principal (there were more than 400,000 suits filed by mid-1995). Most of these suits would fail, but their ability to use the courts and legislatures to make their interests known was a critical part of what Jonathon Fox has called the "thickening of civil society" in Mexico.

Nothing symbolized the plight of El Barzón more poignantly than the bank bail-out that followed the 1994 crisis. The privatization of Mexican banks during the Salinas regime had already produced a series of public scandals – most notably, the failures of Banco Unión and Banco Cremi after it turned out that their new owner, Carlos Cabal Peniche, had bilked the banks of $700 million – though these early problems were minor compared to the situation that faced the banks after the peso crisis. Interest rates in 1995 skyrocketed, owing in part to the fact that the banks' own debts were often in US dollars. Those banks that could not collect on their Mexican debts quickly became insolvent. Amid a wave of foreclosures and a barrage of stories in the news about malfeasance at the banks, public support for any sort of bail-out was not strong.

Yet Zedillo feared that if the banks collapsed, so too would the economy. Early in 1995 he began shoring up the banking system, acquiring the insolvent banks and guaranteeing creditors and depositors. By 1997 twelve of the eighteen privatized banks were back in government hands. The government also assumed the defaulted loans of solvent banks, and invested significant new capital. The private banks received this money with no strings attached; they would never need to repay government largesse.

In December 1998 the PRI and PAN passed a larger bank rescue package, in which the defaulted loans were coalesced under a new bail-out agency, the Bank Savings Protection Fund (FOBAPROA).[15] The auditor hired by FOBAPROA found fraud and improprieties amounting to $7.7 billion in the banks, including $638 million in illegal loans; $4.4 billion in the audited loans involved clear conflicts of interest. Zedillo seemed to brush these facts aside when he proposed that the costs of the bail-out (which ultimately reached $93 billion) be made a part of Mexico's national debt. The PAN and PRD pointed out that many of the debts were illegal loans and demanded specific information about the debts from FOBAPROA. The PRI refused, citing banking privacy laws. Lacking subpoena power, Congress could not investigate.

Zedillo stood firm by his decisions on FOBAPROA, as would Fox after him. The public nevertheless remains angry, a sentiment that is fueled by periodic stories in the press about improprieties in the banking industry. One banker caused a public stir when he revealed that he had funneled $25 million from his banks into the PRI electoral campaigns of 1994. Many were likewise dismayed when Citigroup bought Banamex from Roberto Hernández for $12.5 billion in 2001, with no provision that the government be reimbursed for $3 billion it had granted the bank in the bail-out. And while it is almost certainly true that the stability of these banks has been critical to Mexico's economic growth in recent years, middle-class Mexicans remain convinced that their interests have been sacrificed to support oligarchical powers. Credit for the middle class remains extremely tight, and non-existent for the poor. They are told that they must rely on the market, a market that often seems outrageously skewed in favor of the rich and powerful.

The logic of the market

Under both Zedillo and Fox, the answer to all economic problems seemed to be policies that would accelerate export-led development. Both pressed for more foreign investment in Mexico, and have undertaken specific programs designed to create a more business-friendly environment in the country. Both also tried to open up the energy sector of the economy to private investment. Fox also attempted to extend privatization to the provision of water. Public sentiment heavily opposes privatization, yet the business sector and many in the PAN and the technocratic wing of the PRI believe that inefficiencies, high costs, and poor service in these sectors act as brakes on economic growth (energy costs for business in Mexico are among the highest in the industrial world). In an effort to solve this problem, Zedillo permitted private companies to build electricity plants to meet their own needs, and allowed them to sell their surpluses to other companies. As a result of these reforms, about 35 percent of the electricity in Mexico is now produced by private (generally foreign) companies. Fox also opened up the Burgos Basin in northern Mexico to gas exploration by private companies, but the poor geological data provided by PEMEX and an unfavorable rate of return led to few bids for the right to work in the region.

PEMEX remains a problem for the Mexican government. The company accounts for one-third of the government's budget – and with increased global oil prices PEMEX alone has accounted for a considerable portion of Mexico's recent economic growth. Nevertheless, company officials claim that the government takes most of the company's foreign export earnings to fund the treasury, leaving relatively little for investment in aging infrastructure (including thirty-year-old pipelines) and exploration. Company officials claim that there is a danger that PEMEX will collapse if they do not receive a larger share of their earnings.[16] Oil spills and accidents have plagued the company recently.

Critics of the status quo argue that a more efficient energy sector – an energy sector with private investment – would generate more jobs, not just in energy production but throughout the economy. Privatization would also generate more profits and investment in the economy, and would in the long run produce more revenue for the government. This revenue would come not just in the form of royalties, but in tax receipts throughout the economy. Nationalists counter that oil, gas, and electricity are national patrimonies, and that private investment would benefit only a select few, while profits from Mexican oil would be increasingly exported from the country (as they were in the past). Nationalists tend to gloss over the question of corruption within the energy sector – in some cases in the billions of dollars – by claiming that, with all its flaws, PEMEX is still a critical source of wealth for all Mexicans. To even suggest that Mexico's oil patrimony, hard won through revolution and direct confrontation with the imperial north, should be allowed to once again fall into foreign hands is to defame the nation. For these reasons, all efforts to have PEMEX activities opened to private investors have run into political roadblocks. The PAN remains committed to the private sector, and while the PRI has just recently come out in favor of private investment in the energy sector, PRI leaders demand that oil and electricity remain under government control. The PRD remains resolutely opposed.

Fox's efforts to open up PEMEX to private investment reflect his broader belief that future Mexican prosperity must lie in the expansion of Mexico's business class. His program to spur home ownership among working-class Mexicans, his efforts to promote the creation of small business through micro-credits, and even his

Plan Puebla Panamá (PPP), which is designed to promote economic development in the most impoverished regions of southern Mexico, envision turning Mexico's poor into property owners and business-people.[17] A nation of petit-bourgeois business owners will be more prosperous, more democratic, more stable, and more likely to vote for the PAN.

Given this context, it is perhaps unsurprising that in the same budget in which the final cost of FOBAPROA was set at $93 billion, the federal government allocated $540 million to meet the needs of the poor. Even though the latter figure represented an increase in social spending, this seems like a staggering difference. Clearly, the Mexican state has been able to find the resources it needs to protect and promote the businesses the technocrats view as vital to export-led development. According to this line of reasoning, the banks were not saved because the bank owners were the friends of Mexico's governing elites, but because the banks were too vital to Mexico's macro-economic well-being to be allowed to fail.

The poor, on the other hand, are not particularly vital to the new economy. Lacking the ability to be significant consumers of Mexican manufactured goods, they are interchangeable units of production at best, and obstacles to economic growth at worst, and will prosper or suffer mostly according to the dictates of the market. It is thus unsurprising that the social programs that they depend on should have suffered a similar fate. In the past fifteen years the Mexican state has introduced the logic of the market into social security reform, healthcare reform, and major reforms to the educational system, justifying these initiatives as a means of turning inefficient and corrupt programs into effective undertakings that serve the public interest (by being private). The pesos poor Mexicans have put into private pensions have indeed served the public interest, paying for roads, airports, and other infrastructure. Whether or not they will ever see this money in the form of pension benefits remains an open question.

Troubling signs

But here is the rub. Market liberalization was supposed to promote a steady stream of growth, mostly through manufacturing exports. Since 2002, however, industrial jobs have been leaving Mexico: 700,000 *maquila* jobs were created in the first seven years after NAFTA came into effect, employment peaked in October 2000, and since then 500 of Mexico's 3,700 *maquilas* have closed down, and 300,000 jobs in the sector have been lost, mostly to China. Electronics and textiles have suffered the most; 325 of the 1,222 *maquilas* that made clothing closed between 2001 and 2004.

It is not just lower wages but a series of inefficiencies and costs in the Mexican economy, that are driving jobs overseas. Businessmen complain that in contrast to China, where manufacturers benefit from tax breaks, a strong base of suppliers, well-trained engineers, professional management, and good ports, Mexico offers them high taxes, high input costs, poor services, too much crime, too much bureaucracy, and a shortage of skilled workers. Chinese companies have mastered the just-in-time delivery system that is critical to the US economy more effectively than the Mexicans. Since joining the WTO in 2001, China has nearly matched Mexico in exports to the US of automobiles and parts, electronics and appliances, and has surpassed Mexico in a number other commodities. China now provides 15 percent of the textiles sold in the US, while Mexico provides only 12 percent. Chinese goods are also flooding the Mexican market, further hurting Mexican business. Mexico's small electronics industry, which has struggled since the GATT came into effect, is in danger of complete collapse owing to Chinese imports. If you purchase a statue of the Virgin of Guadalupe in a Mexican market today, there is a good chance that it was made in China.

Mexican business leaders claim that in order to compete they need lower taxes, better infrastructure, and better efforts to curb corruption. They also point to failures by the Mexican government to improve education,[18] and the continued presence of the state in the energy sector. When subsidies are taken into account, fuel, electricity, air fares, highway tolls, and telecommunications remain expensive in Mexico relative to other OECD members. One result is that outside of labor costs, the cost of doing business in Mexico is fairly high.

Even if the Mexican government adopted the proposals of the business community, and was able to revitalize the *maquila* sector, the results would not necessarily be worth the effort. Critics point out that, as a whole, the *maquilas* have always had an ambiguous impact on the Mexican economy. Nearly two-thirds of the work done in *maquilas* involves the assembly of parts imported from the US and then immediately exported. In some sectors the proportion is higher; imported components account for 85 to 95 percent of all vehicles exported to the States. One result is that the impact of *maquilas* on Mexico's trade balance has not been particularly favorable. Furthermore, the ancillary benefits of industrial production – most notably the benefits to suppliers and smaller manufacturers seen in most industrial economies– do not accompany *maquila* production.

Imports have been so critical to industrial production that the export of manufactured products has not kept pace with the import of those same products in recent years. This, along with repeated infusions of foreign capital in Mexico, has produced a consistent deficit in Mexico's current account balance, and has caused total external debt (public and private) to increase. Even as exports grew from $41.2 billion to $166.4 billion between 1991 and 2000, imports grew from $50.3 billion to $174.5 billion. During this time Mexico never once ran a current account surplus, and generally ran a current account deficit of between $10 and $20 billion (between 2 and 3 percent of GDP). This tendency continues; Mexico ran a trade deficit of $8.5 billion on exports of $189 billion in 2004, in spite of a 14.7 percent rise in exports from 2003. When these numbers are broken down, we see that *maquila* production and oil accounted for 86 percent of Mexican exports, valued at $136.3 billion and $23.7 billion respectively. Raw materials, destined mostly for *maquilas*, accounted for the largest category of imports ($149 billion). Machinery and capital goods accounted for $22.6 billion in imports, and $25.4 billion fell into the category "luxury goods."

These are troubling trends, and suggest that the current emphasis on the export of manufactured goods is unsustainable in the long run. Reformers suggested that export-led economic growth would end the trade imbalance, but instead it has spiraled. Private debt in Mexico was $9.04 billion in 1990; by 2001 it was over $54 billion. Currently public and private foreign debt total nearly $150 billion. In recent years payments on the debt exceeded payments on education and health combined.

Mexico's macroeconomic performance offers yet other reasons for alarm. Since the early 1990s the Mexican economy has grown at an average of 3.3 percent, a performance that compares well to the US, but is much lower than the 6.6 percent average growth rate of the period between 1940 and 1965. GDP per capita grew at only 1.3 percent per year in the period 1991–2000, which compares poorly to the period from 1951 to 1980, when it expanded at an average rate of 3.3 percent. Most economists characterize this as sluggish growth at best, and warn that this is inadequate to provide jobs for the millions of Mexicans who enter the workforce every year. Mexico's labor force is expected to grow at 2.3 percent annually in coming decades, and the country needs a growth rate of between 6–7 percent (and, under the current model, a 30 percent annual growth in exports) in order to prevent rising unemployment.

Unemployment in Mexico in 2005 was measured at 3.78 percent (or 1.3 million workers), the highest rate since 1997, in spite of a growth in GDP of 4 percent in 2004. These figures are distorted because the government considers anyone who works even a few hours per week as employed. Moreover, most of the workers who have found jobs since Fox took office are employed in the informal sector, which has increased by over 50 percent since 2000. More than 11 million Mexicans, or one-quarter of the labor force, now make their living in this sector, contributing 12.2 percent of GDP. They sell on the streets, work in the black market, and pay little or no tax. Their numbers are almost as large as the 12.5 million workers who earn benefits through the IMSS.

Mexicans cannot turn to domestically oriented manufacturers, suppliers and business networks to solve these problems, because even though they constitute half of the country's economy, they are in a poor position to prosper under the current economic model. Small and mid-size firms remain for the most part excluded from the export sector, and lack the supports for technology, expert management, distribution, product development, quality control, packaging, and marketing that are available to the big firms. They can find few sources of investment and little government aid, and face a credit market where most resources are devoted to the export sector, driving up the cost of credit for local producers. They are also squeezed by a tight monetary policy aimed at containing inflation and maintaining macroeconomic stability, and a banking sector that has been badly mismanaged since privatization, and thus starved of the resources they need for a transition to an international marketplace (export firms, by contrast, have access to international capital).

Tight government budgets have also limited the public sector's ability to stimulate growth and demand, or aid in capital formation. High unemployment and low wages exacerbate a vicious circle of economic crises, as they tend to depress the demand for goods provided by local producers. Small and medium domestic producers, who along with agriculture employ half of Mexico's workforce, have thus been unable to maintain stable wages and unable to meet the employment demands of a growing population. The export sector has also not stimulated local demand as much as one might think, as recent increases in production have come more from improved productivity than increased employment.

Mexico's current economic program also promises further erosions in an already fragile environment. Under NAFTA Mexican officials were compelled to tighten environmental regulations, and have undertaken some green initiatives in recent times, but export-led development has mostly had a negative effect on the nation's ecosystems. Regulations often go unenforced, the victims of bribes and a desperate need to pursue profitability and low costs. Mexican forests continue to be logged at an alarming rate, in spite of the protests of local peasants-turned-environmentalists, who wind up murdered or jailed on trumped-up charges if they try to fight the timber interests. If the Plan Puebla Panamá goes forward, we can expect more of the same.

Water is perhaps the most threatened resource in this already arid nation (Mexico has less drinking water per capita than Egypt). Commercial agriculture and *maquilas* consume water at an increasingly frenetic pace, and the signs that Mexicans may face a water catastrophe associated with market-based growth are everywhere. Today 12 million Mexicans have no access to drinking water unless it is brought to their communities on trucks, a luxury most cannot afford. Where drinking water is available, it is rarely safe. Seventy-three percent of Mexico's water is contaminated, and the system for cleaning water is failing (none of Chiapas's thirteen treatment plants is functioning). In Mexico City water is pumped from over 100 miles away. The result, when this is combined with the ill effects of airborne pollution (Mexico City remains one of the most polluted places on earth, with not just industrial and auto emissions, but several tons of pulverized fecal matter floating in the air, making it one of the few places on earth where one can inhale hepatitis or dysentery), is that millions of Mexicans live in increasingly unhealthy places. Those with the resources can drink bottled water (Mexico is the second largest consumer of bottled water in the world) or move to outlying communities and suburbs. Others must simply sacrifice their health for the limited economic options they find in the capital.

Conclusion

Defenders of the current system, including the World Bank, agree that these are real problems, but argue both that NAFTA has brought real benefits, and that Mexico's economy would be in far worse shape without the market reforms undertaken since the 1980s. They ask the critics to remember the crises that the Mexican economy faced during the 1980s, and counsel patience in the face of current problems. As long as the economy grows, as long as the currency remains relatively stable and inflation under control, there remains the possibility that the benefits of trade liberalization will ultimately be enjoyed by most Mexicans.

This promise rings hollow to many poor and middle-class Mexicans, who feel an acute contempt for the technocratic elites and powerful interests that created NAFTA. They often characterize globalization as a struggle between the sell-outs and the *jodidos*, with the former representing the current Mexican state that has been selling off the national patrimony to a small foreign-oriented elite, and the latter representing the true Mexican nation. Those members of the elite and middle class who are fortunate enough to live in the dollar economy live in a borderless world. They have papers and look prosperous, and have no need to evade US immigration officials. They travel between Mexico City, New York, and Madrid to shop and work, send their children to US universities, and can shield themselves from the deteriorating conditions of the welfare state by opting for private health, education, and social services. Those middle-class Mexicans who traditionally tied their well-being to the domestic economy are left to scramble to get on board the globalization bandwagon, but most find that the opportunities offered by economic openings are beyond their reach.

For working-class Mexicans, NAFTA's promises remain locked in the distant future. At the moment they are forced to compete in a labor market where wages have been stagnant for almost a decade, even in the most prosperous sectors of the export economy. Those who traditionally made a living in the countryside find that their markets have disappeared, and have been thrown onto a labor market that cannot provide enough jobs for those who need them. Their only option involves following the fruits of Mexican labor northwards in search of work in the US. Economists believe that the free movement of people is part of free market economics; labor power relocates to where it can be best compensated, generating efficiencies. Unfortunately the US government does not see it the same way.

In spite of all of this, polls suggest that almost 80 percent of Mexicans believe that the country's interests lie with the US, rather than with Latin America. This sentiment does not reflect an absence of visceral hostility to the United States; Mexicans continue to nurture a powerful nationalism rooted in part in anti-Americanism, and protest US foreign policy in Latin America and abroad with real fervor. What it instead reflects is pragmatism on the part of the majority of Mexicans, who believe that, in spite of their personal antipathies, their country must collaborate more closely with the US in order to secure its future. Given the experience of many Mexicans under NAFTA this may seem strange, and it is certainly not what populists (Hugo Chávez of Venezuela, for example) want to hear. Nevertheless, it reflects the complex logic that informs the experiences of most Mexicans in this day and age. A close relationship with the USA (and globalization more generally) may portend a difficult future, but it seems the best of a series of poor options.

7 | Conclusion: democracy in Mexico

During the cold war Western politicians took for granted the fact that market-based capitalism and democracy were intimately linked concepts. An open economy, this belief went, in turn produced an open society. Nearly two decades after Tiananmen Square we know that this is not true, that democratic and economic reform may be linked, but that those connections are neither transparent nor inevitable. For Mexicans, this means that whatever the results of economic reform, political reform needs a spirit of its own, an impulse to protect and expand the democratic rights of Mexican citizens that is not dependent on economic factors. Mexicans understand that if the poor grow increasingly desperate under the current system their fragile democracy cannot survive, yet they do not tend to believe that democracy derives simply from material circumstances. Democracy is rather a complex, often idiosyncratic series of processes that must flourish in and of themselves.

Mexican democracy did not spring entirely from local origins; it is deeply linked to larger global phenomena. The global technological and communications revolutions of the last quarter-century have profoundly impacted Mexican political processes. The very languages of opposition movements – dirty wars, indigenous self-determination, environmentalism, human rights, and clean elections – are drawn from a variety of global movements that have flourished in recent decades. Democratic agitators also consciously built their movements with an eye to the outside world, relying on support from abroad, living and studying in foreign countries, and creating powerful networks that ignored the frontier. These practices made it impossible for the state to use its traditional mechanisms to stifle dissent, and ultimately undermined the fiction that had for generations linked nationalism and authoritarianism. Those networks also promoted the growth of non-governmental organizations

(NGOs) in Mexican life, and helped provide the foreign observers who ensured increased transparency in the 1994 and 2000 elections. Using their new-found resources to agitate for change, migrants too have forged crucial openings, and can now vote in presidential elections even while they reside abroad.

That said, several critical questions continue to confound the young Mexican democracy. Democratic processes are in place, but are not always respected. Process can prove inadequate if torture, murder, intimidation, and vote-buying continue to characterize Mexican politics. Women, more than 50 percent of the population, remain under-represented and disadvantaged. Gays, lesbians, bi-sexuals, and transvestites live in fear of brutality, knowing full well that few Mexicans will sympathize with their plight. Indigenous Mexicans, the poorest sector in society, have seen little progress in their bid for rights. Most of all, though, for the more than half of Mexicans who have been the losers in globalization, Mexican democracy often seems like a clever farce, an opportunity to vote for the man who will invariably make your life more difficult. Many millions of Mexicans voted for change and felt the "Romance of Democracy" (Gutmann 2002) in 2000, but as with most romances, they fear a tragic ending.

Processes

In rather sharp contrast to its northern neighbor, Mexico looked like a fairly functional democracy in the 2000 elections. After 2000 the PRI, PAN, and PRD could each claim a significant share of power at the federal, state, and local levels, and since none held an absolute majority in Congress, it was virtually impossible to maintain the authoritarian practices of the past. Fox took this reality into account when he created his cabinet, drawing politicians from left and right in an effort to build a workable coalition based on transparency, an end to corruption and nepotism, and a respect for basic human rights and freedoms.[1]

Within a few months of his inauguration, Mexicans could see that the absolute presidency had become a relic of the past, replaced by a gridlocked political system. Hemmed in by Congress and an increasingly assertive judiciary, Fox had little power over the other branches of government. Even PAN supporters (*panistas*) openly criticized Fox. They attacked his cabinet for marginalizing party members (only 19 percent of Fox's top fifty appointments were from the PAN) and refused to press his agenda in Congress. Fox was able to make good on a few promises (he successfully pushed legislation requiring more transparency in government contracts and the federal budget), but the reform agenda had ground to a halt by 2002. Congress even obstructed foreign policy, delaying ratification of the International Criminal Court in 2002, and refusing Fox permission to travel to the US and Canada in mid-2002 because he had criticized the Cuban government.

The Mexican Congress has never had much of a reputation for responsible behavior, in part because the prohibition against re-election to any office offers little incentive for accountability. In the past, this tendency was tempered because the Congress simply rubber-stamped presidential initiatives, but under Fox the lack of party discipline produced a tendency to capriciousness. Governors and municipal leaders, many of whom saw their budgets rise three-fold because of the decentralization of government, and who faced little accountability, also suddenly found that they could exert as much (or more) influence on Congress as the president (in part because they could hire deputies at the end of their terms).[2]

After a brief spike in approval when he refused to support the US invasion of Iraq, Fox reached his nadir with the 2003 mid-term elections. In the July 6 elections the PAN lost fifty-four seats in the Chamber of Deputies, falling to 151, while the PRI expanded from 208 to 222, and the PRD nearly doubled from fifty-four to ninety-five. In 2004 and 2005 the plural nature of Mexico's multi-party democracy was reaffirmed by electoral victories at the state level for all three parties. The PAN won critical elections in Tlaxcala and the Yucatán, expanding their power into new regions. The PRD won elections in Baja California Sur and Zacatecas, and a critical election in Guerrero, where in February 2005 Zeferino Torreblanca Galindo was elected the first ever non-PRI governor of the state. Guerrero has a long-held reputation for political violence, but the election took place peacefully.

These victories should not be taken as signs that the PRI is on the verge of collapse. In 2004 and 2005 the PRI won elections in Coahuila, Mexico State, Puebla, Tamaulipas, Sinaloa, Oaxaca, and Veracruz. Under the leadership of Roberto Madrazo, the strident party insider who refused to back down when confronted by Zedillo, a "reformed PRI" promises to embrace democracy while returning to its populist roots. Some in the PRI remain uncomfortable about Madrazo's history of political abuses and suspicious practices in several recent elections, but his rejection of the recent technocratic past helped the party win a majority of gubernatorial contests between 2003 and 2005. The PRI also saw gains in some PAN strongholds in the north, reclaiming the mayor's office in Tijuana and Ciudad Juárez.

Anticipating a tight election in 2006, Mexico's major parties are in the process of raising over $1 billion for the campaigns. It is lost on no one that this amount dwarfs federal spending on anti-poverty programs, and threatens to distort the process, as candidates in effect purchase editorial views as they purchase advertising in the major media. Mexico's campaign finance laws are proving difficult to enforce, and a variety of illicit campaign contributions seem to be finding their way to all parties. The IFE has tried to level the playing field by offering to match private contributions given to the eight major parties as long as spending caps are observed, but this has had little effect.

The highly competitive nature of Mexico's new political system may not have yielded significant legislative results, but it has produced more political scandals than the country has ever seen. Mexican politicians have discovered that their critics (whether opportunistic or ideological) have an entirely new arsenal of weapons in the struggle for power. The list of victims of the political opening is vast. The leader of the Green Party was involved in scandal in 2004 when his son was caught negotiating bribes in return for permits for commercial development in the Yucatán. Marta Sahagún (Fox's wife) has been investigated because of allegations that her two sons from a previous marriage used their connections to win construction contracts valued at $228 million. She has also faced questions about the size of her staff, which includes thirty-eight aides. In February 2005 Nahum Acosta Lugo, an aide to President Fox, was arrested on suspicion of passing information to Joaquín Guzmán Loera's drugs cartel. The aide was later released for lack of evidence.

The PRD has also been stung by a series of scandals since 2000, most of them surrounding Andrés Manuel López Obrador, who was mayor of Mexico City from 2000 to 2005. López Obrador publicly reduced his salary and moved into a modest residence after his election to the mayor's office, but quickly discovered that public transparency laws would give his opponents ammunition for their attacks. Much of the symbolism of his public sacrifice was lost with the news that his friend and chauffeur, Nicolás Mollinedo, was earning a monthly salary of nearly $6,000, fifteen times the salary of the other chauffeurs working for the city, and equivalent to salaries earned by top city officials. López Obrador was further stung in 2004 when Carlos Ahumada, a city contractor, was filmed delivering large sums of money to city officials, and when Mexico City's chief of finance, Gustavo Ponce, was filmed living the high life at the Bellagio Hotel in Las Vegas, betting large sums of money and incurring an enormous tab, all with public funds. Ahumada was arrested in Cuba in March 2004. Ponce was arrested in Tepoztlán, Morelos, in October 2004. He was charged with money laundering.

The effect of these scandals paled beside the events that threatened to derail the presidential ambitions of Andrés Manuel López Obrador in early 2005. At a time when polls suggested that as many as 43 percent of Mexicans would vote for López Obrador for president in 2006 (making him three times as popular as the nearest contender), the PRI and PAN came together in an effort to bar him from running for the post. They found cause to derail his campaign in an incident from 2004, when he ignored a court order and allowed the construction of a hospital access road over private land in Mexico City. López Obrador enjoyed immunity from prosecution as mayor, but if he were stripped of immunity he could be charged with contempt of court. If charged, he would be forbidden from running for president while the matter was pending.

No Mexican politician had ever been charged over such a minor transgression, but on April 1, 2005, a coalition of 360 PRI and PAN law-makers voted to strip López Obrador of immunity. Fox hailed the vote as a sign that elected officials were no longer above the law. Critics throughout the country and around the world cried foul. The nakedly political nature of the prosecution seemed all the more clear in light of the fact that even as they went after López Obrador the PRI blocked any action against PRI senator Ricardo Aldena in the Pemexgate scandal (Aldena was directly involved in a scheme that diverted $127 million from PEMEX to the 2000 PRI campaigns).

In the weeks after April 1 hundreds of thousands of protesters marched through Mexico City's streets. The crowd swelled to 750,000 on April 24, after Fox pressed charges. López Obrador reveled in the spotlight, imploring his supporters to eschew violence, and promising to run for president from jail if necessary. At the height of the conflict, polls indicated that 60 percent of Mexicans saw the prosecution as a political conspiracy to keep him from office. Fox made matters worse by trying to charge López Obrador without arresting him, in effect denying him the symbolic capital that an arrest would confer. A judge rejected these efforts, reasoning that López Obrador needed to be arrested in order to be charged. Just days later the case collapsed, and on April 27 Attorney General Rafael Macedo de la Concha resigned. Fox then dropped the case.

Within weeks of the resolution of the López Obrador case, the government banned former PEMEX director Rogelio Montemayor Seguy and five other former PEMEX officials from holding public office for between five and twenty years, and fined them $255 million for the Pemexgate scandal. *Priistas* claimed that the fine, coming so shortly on the heels of the López Obrador case, was a sign of an agreement between Fox and PRD to go after the PRI. In turn they launched investigations against Santiago Creel, who was then the leading PAN contender for the presidency in 2006, accusing him of granting gambling licenses to television networks in exchange for heavily discounted airtime for his campaign advertisements.

The maelstrom of attacks and counter-attacks is overwhelming, and would make it easy to dismiss the new Mexican politics as a blood sport. To be sure, there is a risk that the current scandal-mongering tendency of Mexican politics will favor a new and newly authoritarian PRI; this is something that Roberto Madrazo seems to be counting on. He has managed to build up his political networks in spite of his anti-democratic image, relying on the PRI tradition of delivering the goods, and an image as a strong disciplined leader to sway voters in critical elections. And yet there is reason to think that Madrazo may be naïve to think that he can return the system to its old ways. He may be missing the fact that inasmuch as the scandals make Mexican politicians look bad, they also reveal that a tightly controlled political system has given way to a profoundly pluralistic civil society. It is now impossible to get away with the things that politicians used to do habitually, even though many seem to be learning this fact only slowly. The messiness of the process suggests something about the complexity of the transformation; Mexican politics is neither uniformly corrupt nor uniformly transparent, and it may take decades for the full repercussions of transparency to become clear. But the sheer number of voices in the contest – and the thickening of civil society that these voices represent – suggests a change that will not be undone. Only one thing is certain: more than one Mexican politician wishes that videotape had never been invented.

The specter of human rights

The claim to human rights has proved to be a powerful and deeply symbolic tool in Mexico's democratic transition.[3] Perhaps more than anything else, a Fox presidency promised to uncover abuses that the PRI had long kept hidden because of its stranglehold on the system. During the campaign Fox promised wholesale changes; he would put a stop to the militarization of policing, he would abolish the Attorney General's Office, he would hold prosecutors to account for their abuses, and he would end the use of torture and fabricated evidence in criminal cases. More than this, he would call the PRI, the military, and the police to account for decades of abuse.

As with Fox's other heady promises, most of these expectations would be impossible to fulfill. He quickly learned that without the attorney general he might lose control of the country. He even appointed a former general as attorney general, directly repudiating his promise to reduce the military role in policing.[4] Human rights reform would require cooperation from Congress, which he could not count on. Moreover, if he wanted to stop abuses, he would need the help of thousands of state and municipal police agents throughout the country, most of whom were not under his jurisdiction.

In the short run, Fox was able to take two important steps. First, he reversed decades of federal policy by inviting human rights observers from the UN, Amnesty International (AI), and a host of other NGOs to enter the country, reversing Zedillo's practice of expelling foreign activists. These men and women were given the opportunity to document abuses in ways that had never before been possible, and created new pressures for reform. Second, he appointed a special prosecutor to investigate the past abuses of Mexico's government, opening the way for a full accounting of Mexico's dirty war, and not incidentally offering the opportunity to embarrass the PRI.

Fox proceeded slowly, but a variety of civic organizations did not let the process stall. Public pressure produced Mexico's first Freedom of Information Law, which Fox signed on June 10, 2002. A week later Fox held a public ceremony at the National Archives where he released 60,000 secret police, military, and intelligence records from the 1950s to the 1980s. The released documents revealed that between 1968 and 1985, 482 people were kidnapped and murdered by the government. They also provided a great deal of evidence about two massacres that held special significance for Mexicans, the massacre at Tlatelolco and the massacre of twenty-five student demonstrators during a demonstration in Mexico City on June 10, 1971. For those who had lived through the massacres and who had finally come into positions of power, these two events were linked by the personage of Luis Echeverría Álvarez, interior minister in 1968, and president in 1971. Echeverría was not directly implicated in any murders by the documents, but they revealed enough about his role in organizing the Halcones for prosecutors to decide to charge him with genocide.

Early efforts to bring charges were hindered by the statute of limitations, but in November 2003 the Supreme Court ruled that charges could be filed in the case of "disappearances" where no body had been found. This decision led to a wave of arrest warrants against former officials, including the eighty-three-year-old Echeverría and his interior minister, Mario Augusto Moya Palencia. Two years of legal wrangling followed, but all the charges were eventually dismissed in July 2005, when a judge ruled that there was insufficient evidence to pursue the case. Later efforts to charge Echeverría with the 1968 Tlatelolco massacre similarly came to naught.

Falling short of a legal victory, the cases against Echeverría were nonetheless a symbolic victory for past victims of abuse, and a political victory for the PAN and PRD. Beyond this, however, these developments mean very little to the thousands of Mexicans who continue to suffer from the routine denial of human rights. Between 1990 and 2004, the CNDH received 84,689 complaints, and documented 588 cases of torture.[5] Both the UN and AI allege that torture is common in Mexico, and used by all branches of the security forces. Evidence obtained through torture is routinely used in criminal cases, in spite of constitutional prohibitions against torture and cruel, inhuman, and degrading punishment. In the past, these practices were critical to maintaining the authority of the PRI. Today these agencies no longer keep the PRI in power on a national level, but police agencies still serve a variety of powerful interests, going after political enemies when called upon. Fox has little power over these arrangements; he cannot buy the police off, he cannot fire them, and he cannot simply demand transparency. Ordinary Mexicans know this all too well, and often live in fear of their lives when confronting the police. Neither are prominent activists immune.

Mexicans were shocked and dismayed by the death of Digna Ochoa on October 19, 2001. Ochoa was a prominent human rights lawyer who had uncovered several cases of military and police torture. The thirty-seven-year-old former nun, who worked with the Jesuit-run Miguel Agustin Pro Juárez Human Rights Center (PRODH), was found dead in her office, having been shot twice, once in the leg and once in the head. An anonymous note found near her body threatened further attacks on human rights activists. Prosecutors declared the death a suicide, claiming that she shot herself first in the leg, then fell to her knees, put the gun in her other hand, and shot herself in the head. The fact that the shot to her head seemed to come from above her was left unexplained. Family members were horrified by the finding, especially since Ochoa had been the subject of repeated threats. Mexican investigators ultimately reopened the investigation in 2005, but few Mexicans have confidence that there will be a fair resolution.

The sheer bravado of police malfeasance in the denial of human rights has been most starkly on display in a murder spree in Chihuahua that has lasted for more than a decade. The murders first came to light in 1993, when the body of thirteen-year-old Alma Chavira Farel was found raped, beaten, and strangled in an empty lot. Bodies of young women started appearing in and around Juárez and Chihuahua City at regular intervals thereafter. The women tended to be dark-skinned, with long hair, and were almost invariably poor workers in *maquilas*. Most were killed as they traveled between their homes in poor *barrios* and their jobs, often commuting after dark in places with little or no police presence. A significant number of the corpses have also shown evidence of sexual assault.

In Juárez in particular, where almost half of the population of 1.5 million are migrants drawn to the city to work in the *maquilas*, the poor, recent migrants who live in the shanty towns who ring the city make perfect victims. Race and class prejudice rendered these murders unimportant; early on police and the general public dismissed the victims as loose women or prostitutes. Inaction by the police allowed the killing spree to accelerate, so that to this date the bodies of approximately four hundred women have been found.

When public pressure mounted and the police needed to solve a crime or two, they would simply round up someone suspicious, sometimes a family member, and then torture them until they confessed. Torture was used to elicit confessions to eight murders from the bus driver Victor "El Cerrillo" García Uribe. Arrested in 2001, he was repeatedly denied access to counsel, and his lawyer was threatened by officials and later killed by state police. In 2004 he was sentenced to fifty years in prison, despite the fact that he recanted a confession made under torture. García's alleged accomplice, fellow bus driver Gustavo González, died under suspicious circumstances in prison in 2003. García Uribe had to wait three and a half years for his release, which came when Chihuahua's State Supreme Court overturned his conviction in June 2005. By contrast, when the former state judicial official Hector Lastra was arrested for leading a prostitution ring that forcibly recruited under-age girls who often fit the profile of the victims, he was quickly released on bail.

The crimes committed in Chihuahua were under the jurisdiction of local officials, and two governors and their attorney generals insisted that it remain that way. When victims' families criticized local police for botched investigations, and even accused police of being involved, state officials responded with threats against the victims' families. Ignoring these threats, the victims' families turned to national and international NGOs for aid, spreading news of the murders north of the border in the late 1990s. American media and NGOs were somewhat slow to respond, but in the next few years a trickle of news stories gradually produced a wave of public interest north of the border.

Mexico's own CNDH did not release a report on the murders until November 2003, three months after AI released a report condemning official inaction in the Chihuahua murders. Both reports noted that remains had been misidentified, investigations slow, suspects tortured, evidence falsified, and lawyers and families threatened. Also, in the fall of 2003 a US congressional delegation headed by Hilda Solis (D-CA) visited Juárez, after which she introduced a bill in the US Congress condemning the murders and calling for US government action. The end of the year was punctuated by extreme embarrassment for the Mexican government, when Norma Andrade, the mother of Juárez victim Lilia Alejandra García Andrade, testified in the US Congress about the murder spree. In her testimony she accused Chihuahua governor Patricio Martínez of threatening those families that looked for aid from international agencies.

Prompted by the wave of bad press, in October 2003 Fox created a new federal office to investigate the murders. Guadalupe Morfín Otero, head of Jalisco's Human Rights Commission, was appointed Special Federal Commissioner on Violence against Women in Ciudad Juárez.[6] In January 2004 Fox named María López Urbina, a prominent human rights lawyer, as a new special prosecutor, though her mandate was limited to those cases that fell under federal jurisdiction. After reviewing only about fifty cases, López Urbina accused 129 former and current state officials of negligence and dereliction of duty. Eighty-one were charged. López Urbina remained silent about the two former governors, Francisco Barrio of the PAN and Patricio Martínez of the PRI, who are accused by many victims of obstruction and intimidation.

Victims' families have been disappointed that López Urbina's investigations have not focused on the murders, and are angry that the killings do not seem to have abated (at least eighteen women were murdered in Juárez in 2004). No longer willing to wait for federal help, in October 2004 victims' relatives launched a Caravan of Justice to fifty-four US and Canadian cities. Their tour was sponsored by the US-based Mexico Solidarity Network, and included a number of recently created local groups, such as Nuestras Hijas de Regreso a Casa (Return Our Daughters Home) and Justicia para Nuestras Hijas (Justice for Our Daughters). Among their audiences in the US were several congressmen and the Inter-American Commission on Human Rights. When they returned to Mexico, the victims' family members were involuntarily photographed by AFI agents. Some also reported being the victims of police surveillance.

As a result of these murders Mexicans have become familiar with a new word: feminicide. Human rights activists introduced this word into the Mexican lexicon to remind their fellow citizens that attacks on women *because they are women*, the refusal to investigate or take crimes against women seriously, and efforts to intimidate women because of their presumed weakness can all be fairly classified as hate crimes. The cases in Chihuahua may be the most visible, but women's rights groups point out that there has recently been a rise in feminicide in Sonora, Tamaulipas, Coahuila, and Guanajuato. In the first half of 2005 alone, eighteen women in Sonora were killed by their partners. This is one of the few places where these statistics are available, but sources from elsewhere in the country suggest that the phenomenon is widespread. One of the most chilling rumors in Chihuahua is that abusive boyfriends and husbands may have used the cover of the murder spree to kill their partners.

Federal law prohibits domestic violence, but officials need to be willing to enforce these laws for them to have any effect, and the evidence is not encouraging in this regard. Women rarely trust police officials, and almost never turn to police for help. Even when they turn to supposedly sympathetic officials, the record is not good.

In the past five years the CNDH has received almost four thousand complains about offenses against women by federal officials, which probably represents only a fraction of the true number. Most significant were abuse of authority, denial of medical services, threats, and denial of the right to file a complaint.

According to official statistics, 47 percent of Mexican women over the age of fifteen have suffered some form of physical, emotional, or sexual abuse. Abuse is extremely common in the workforce; officials estimate that 80 percent of women in the Mexico City workforce have experienced sexual harassment. Typical of these experiences, in January 2004 an NGO charged that electronics contractors in Guadalajara were recruiting poorly educated women, subjecting them to degrading interviews, interrogating them about their sexual histories and performing invasive physical examinations. These women find it very difficult to have their rights respected, and risk unemployment if they resist illegal efforts to test them (often repeatedly) for pregnancy. Even worse, in some parts of the country women's inequality is enshrined in law. In several states women cannot bring suit to establish paternity, making forced child support impossible unless there is outside evidence (i.e. a conviction for rape).

Gay Mexicans face similar challenges in their demand for rights. In spite of Mexico's increasingly vocal gay rights movement – gay pride and lesbian pride parades now take place every year, Mexico City has had a few openly gay officials, and in 2003 Mexico became only the second country in Latin America to enact anti-discrimination laws that protect people based on their sexual orientation – the dangers faced by homosexuals are acute. The National Commission on Hate Crimes estimates that 900 homosexuals have been murdered in the last ten years. Unlike feminicides, where the murderer is generally known and prosecutions relatively common, homicides of homosexuals are almost never prosecuted. Along with other marginalized groups, gays must often defend their rights without the aid of the state.

Given the history of the Mexican state, it is not surprising that the most marginalized people in the country generally turn to extra-legal means to defend their human rights. The EZLN has repeatedly closed off "rebel territory" to outsiders with the claim that this is the only way to prevent abuses. In other parts of the country, community leaders often do as much as possible to limit the influence of government officials. Mexican police agencies have little or no presence in poorer neighborhoods and communities in much of the country, and are not generally welcome. When they do try to establish a presence, they are sometimes rebuffed violently. On November 23, 2004, two police officers were seized and burned to death by a mob in a Mexico City suburb. Members of the mob thought the plainclothes police were there to kidnap children. The police were in fact there taking pictures as part of a drug investigation. The tragedy underlined the fact that, for all the visceral satisfaction of seeing police fleeing a community and self-defense forces asserting control, the miscarriages of justice and abuses in these instances sometimes rival the worst the Mexican state has to offer.

The federal government remains convinced that the solution to these crises lies in more effective law enforcement, but police and the judiciary need to succeed in two projects if they are ever to gain the trust of the Mexican public. They must reduce human rights violations and corruption, and they must do this with an air of transparency. Towards these ends, in December 2004 Fox unveiled the "National Human Rights Program," the first major federal initiative to coordinate human rights work between the federal government and state and local officials. At the same time he openly committed the government to fighting torture. He sent Congress an initiative to modify Article 20 of the constitution, making confessions inadmissible if not made directly before a judge. This reform would also establish a presumption of innocence, guaranteed access to defense counsel, and provisions that would quash evidence gathered illegally.[7] Even though they would not apply in cases where organized crime was involved, if passed by Congress these reforms will revolutionize the justice system.

Civil society will not need to rely on the Mexican government's claims of an improved record and greater transparency. There are now 5,399 NGOs in the country, including 979 focused specifically on human rights. Their work continues to make abuses more and more difficult to hide. There is also hope for Mexico's increasingly independent judiciary, which still often protects powerful interests but has repeatedly rebuffed government pressure (both PRI and PAN) in recent years. The courage of the journalists who risk and all too often lose their lives exposing both official misconduct and drug trafficking reveals a changed journalistic culture that offers a great deal of hope for the future of civil society. Police forces sometimes still act as if they can abuse the rights of Mexicans with impunity, but the fact that their abuses are increasingly likely to explode into an escalating series of public scandals offers hope that those abuses will become less viable in the long run. For the first time in living memory, some officials are being held to account for violating the human rights of their fellow citizens.

The list of police officers who have been incarcerated for their abuses continues to grow. In the past several years nearly one thousand Mexico City police officials have been charged with crimes. In June 2003 two Tarahumara anti-logging activists who had been arrested on weapons and drugs charges were released from jail, and three officials were charged with planting evidence in their case. In 2004 thirteen Chihuahua state police agents were arrested and warrants were issued for four others, in a case in which the bodies of twelve torture victims were discovered behind a Juárez home. Also in 2004 a federal judge convicted five AFI agents in the 2002 death of Guillermo Vélez Mendoza, who had been arrested by the PGR under suspicion of his involvement in a kidnapping. Even the military is slowly responding, recently reinstating charges against General Arturo Acosta Chaparro in connection with the deaths of twenty-two peasants in the 1970s.

That said, human rights violations comprise such a web of practices that they cannot be easily stopped. If we take just one year – 2004 – and just the most public cases from the year, which no doubt represent a fraction of the human rights violations nationally, we start to see the complex problems Mexico must confront. In January, police in Zapotitlan Tablas, Guerrero, detained and tortured Socrates Tolentino González Genaro, ultimately killing him. When his mother came to collect his body, police had her sign a form. She was illiterate, and did not realize that the form indicated that she accepted police accounts that her son had committed suicide. In May, in Guadalajara, police detained and tortured scores of protesters at a Latin American and Caribbean summit. Over fifty were held incommunicado for two days. Some were even arrested as they sought aid at a Red Cross clinic. There was no investigation. Also in May, police detained, beat, and robbed the journalist Manuel de la Cruz in Tuxtla Gutiérrez, Chiapas. In August, lawyers María del Carmen Grajales and Heriberto Gómez, acting as defense attorneys in a murder case, were charged with fabricating evidence in reprisal for accusing police of fabricating evidence. In September, Guadalupe Avilas Salina, mayoral candidate in San José Estancia Grande, Oaxaca, was murdered by the municipal president, who evaded arrest. In November, Felipe Arriaga, in Petatlán, Guerrero, was jailed on charges that he had murdered the son of a wealthy landowner nearly six years previously, in spite of overwhelming evidence that he had nothing to do with the crime. The arrest was made as a reprisal for Arriaga's efforts to stop logging in his community. He was freed in September 2005. On several occasions during 2004 indigenous leaders in Guerrero and Chiapas were assassinated, mostly by paramilitaries working in conjunction with local elites.

These cases remind us that in spite of all efforts and a growing number of arrests, Mexican police are still willing to use violence and intimidation to hide their activities. Even if Fox's legal reforms are passed, the Mexican state simply does not have the resources or authority to enforce much of their agenda on the ground. The elimination of torture, respect for due process, and the variety of elements constituting the defense of human rights are tied to a vast web of practices and customs that can neither be coerced nor bought. Indeed, resources and coercion may be necessary (given that municipal police officers in Mexico generally earn about $350 per month, and must buy their own bullet-proof vests, handcuffs, and bullets), but the subtle attitudinal changes required must come from somewhere else.

Indigenous self-determination

Indigenous Mexicans face routine violations of their human rights, violations that are so common that they often seem integral to the fabric of daily life in rural Mexico. Local elites have always used threats and intimidation to deny land claims, maintain a constant supply of indigenous laborers, and force indigenous Mexicans into line as their (sometimes unwilling) political support systems.[8] And yet for indigenous Mexicans these acts are often experienced not simply as violations of their personhood, but also as assaults on community institutions and customs. It is because of this that the language of indigenous self-determination found ready adherents among Mexico's indigenous peoples long before the Chiapas uprising.[9] At first the Mexican government was slow to respond to these demands, making limited concessions that recognized indigenous cultures as distinct but never acknowledging a right to autonomy for indigenous peoples. The rebellion in Chiapas changed all this, particularly once the Zapatistas altered their strategy in late 1994 and made indigenous rights their central demand.

After breaking off negotiations in 1994, the government and EZLN began new negotiations in the town of San Andrés Larráinzar in April 1995, and after months of negotiations ultimately agreed to peace accords on February 16, 1996. The accords called for Congress to recognize indigenous communities as public entities organized into autonomous municipalities, which would have the power, among other things, to direct their own development projects and control the implementation of social programs. The accords also called for federal efforts to promote and protect women's rights and interests, bilingual education for indigenous peoples, efforts to meet the basic needs of indigenous communities, and a general program to improve the image of indigenous peoples in Mexico. Perhaps most importantly, the accords called on the government to recognize "indigenous peoples' right to the sustainable use and the derived benefits of the use and development of the natural resources of the territories they occupy or utilize."

This was a remarkable vision, but the accords were dead on arrival in Mexico City. National polls suggested that a significant number of Mexicans, perhaps even a majority, supported the San Andrés Accords, but Congress did not. Zedillo had already lost much of his authority over the PRI delegation in the Congress, and leaders of the PRI and PAN immediately made it quite clear that the accords went much too far in granting indigenous peoples' autonomy and control of their resources. The EZLN withdrew from negotiations in

September, and then went directly to the Mexican public in October, when Comandante Ramona traveled to Mexico City to advocate on behalf of the accords. Further marches on Mexico City and San Cristobal in 1997 yielded no results, and when Zedillo introduced his indigenous law on March 15, 1998, autonomy was limited to the community level. The Zapatistas rejected the law, and withdrew completely from the dialogue.

Zedillo was more effective when it came to harassing Zapatista sympathizers, activists, and journalists. In early 1995, he decided to "unmask" the Zapatista leader and pursue arrest warrants for the EZLN leadership. Mexicans learned that Marcos was Rafael Sebastián Guillén Vicente, the son of a furniture magnate in Tampico, and a former Mexico City academic. In June 1995 the government began expelling foreigners from Chiapas. The military in Chiapas also stepped up its repression in the region, increasing troop deployments and offering tacit support to a growing number of paramilitary groups. The paramilitaries were complex organizations, sometimes in the employ of local landlords and elites, but at other times representing local factions in power struggles with the EZLN. By arming the paramilitaries and then sitting idly by, the government contributed to a dramatic increase in violence in the region. Paramilitaries in the state forcibly recruited some of their members, levied taxes, and used violence to intimidate members of the opposition, sometimes driving people out of their communities and burning their homes.

Their role in the escalating violence made international headlines in late December 1997, when sixty members of a paramilitary group massacred forty-five peasants, including women, children, and infants, in a six-hour slaughter in the village of Acteal. Public Security Police located about 250 meters away never responded to the cries for help. The dead, in a tragic irony, were not even Zapatistas, but members of a group committed to non-violence and neutrality that called itself the "Bees." More than one hundred individuals were charged with the crimes, including PRI officials and police officers.

Four days after the massacre 2,000 soldiers arrived in the municipality, and within a year more than 70,000 troops could be found in the state. During this period Zedillo pressed for an alternative to the

San Andrés Accords, and police arrested several Zapatista and other indigenous leaders and expelled an increasing number of foreigners from the region. Army soldiers also dismantled Zapatista structures in a number of the autonomous municipalities. Large-scale movements of sometimes more than a thousand soldiers confronted stick- and stone-wielding Zapatistas in Ricardo Flores Magon (April 11), Amparao Aguatinta (May 1), Nicolas Ruiz (May 5) and Chavajebal (June 13), dismantling Zapatista offices, beating protesters, and arresting dozens. In Chavajebal several people were killed when the police used bazookas against protesters. In another, at Union Progreso, police allegedly executed seven peasants as they demonstrated peacefully. The state government took this as an opportunity to forcibly disband several autonomous municipalities.

This slowly bleeding stalemate was supported by the right wing of the PAN and PRI, who feared the bad publicity of an all-out campaign to retake rebel territory but rejected the San Andrés Accords because they would threaten the land tenure of a number of powerful interests and possibly prevent the further development of the Lacandón forest's timber, mineral, and petroleum reserves. They could also count on the intransigence of the EZLN to justify the stalemate. As long as the EZLN refused to return to the bargaining table, and refused to participate in a progressively more open political process, they seemed out of touch with the Mexican mainstream, a violent and intransigent relic of another time.

During the late 1990s the EZLN grew in stature as heroes for the international left. Thousands of foreign activists, journalists, and tourists descended on Chiapas to meet the revolutionaries, drawn by the mysterious aura of Marcos and the appeal of Zapatista declarations on indigenous rights, women's rights, the environment and, most notably, their position in the war against globalization. Riding the wave of international celebrity, in April 1996 the Zapatistas hosted a series of international forums that featured dignitaries from more than forty countries. They met with representatives of Argentina's Madres de la Plaza de Mayo, Régis Debray, Oliver Stone, Danielle Mitterrand, Alain Touraine, Saul Landau, and Eduardo Galeano. Speaking at one encounter, Alain Touraine summarized the Zapatista appeal to global activists.

I believe that international opinion appreciates a great deal of what the Indian communities of Chiapas are – located in a space, a time, a culture, they speak a universal language. In some way the ski masks signify "we are you," the universality. I am at the same time a member of my community but with the voice of my mountain I speak with the phrase, *I am you*. That, along with the phrase *to command while obeying*, is the greatest definition of what is democracy.

Perhaps lost on Touraine was the fact that the ski masks signified more precisely a desire to avoid detection by the authorities, or the fact that there was often much commanding within the EZLN, but very little obeying. More problematic still for Mexicans was the way in which local conflict over land and power had become linked to a series of loquacious philosophers and movements to which most Mexicans did not feel connected. Oliver Stone may have admired the Zapatistas as defiant rebels, but by 1996 most Mexicans wanted the EZLN to lay down their arms, form a political party, and enter the national political arena.

Matters gradually grew worse for the Zapatistas as a force within Mexican politics. As the rest of the country moved toward the 2000 elections, the Zapatistas refused to lay down their arms, and continued to issue a steady stream of sometimes bizarre declarations from the jungle. Outsiders were increasingly unwelcome in the thirty-eight rebel municipalities, in which about 10 percent of the 700,000 indigenous peoples in the state live. The EZLN forbade the entry of doctors and nurses from the government health service, census takers, teachers, agronomists, and the like. The Zapatistas even rebuffed efforts by TELMEX to install phone lines. The result only exacerbated the physical suffering in the regions they controlled.

Reports about Zapatistas expelling villagers who did not support the EZLN diminished their stature among Mexicans further. Expulsions were not unique to the Zapatistas, and had been a problem in indigenous communities in Chiapas since the 1970s (previously, it was mostly the expulsion of Protestants), but evidence of human rights abuses committed by the EZLN had given the uprising an increasingly ambiguous cast by the late 1990s. National polls continued to show that a significant number of Mexicans supported some form of self-determination for indigenous peoples, but as the public became more aware that indigenous peoples were also violators of indigenous human rights, self-determination lost some of its appeal as a simple solution to the oppression of indigenous peoples. The passage of time also revealed that Zapatista declarations about gender equity, the occupation of land since time immemorial, and democracy within the movement were fantasies concocted to inspire the popular imagination and not established facts, further tarnishing the romance of the uprising.

The ambiguities of the struggle became tragically clear in the investigations of the massacre in Acteal. The roots of the massacre, it turned out, lay in a 1997 power struggle between Zapatistas and *priistas* over control of the municipality of Chenalhó. The *priistas* won the power struggle, but in the village of Polhó the Zapatistas nevertheless tried to take power. The results were a series of running battles during the year, in which twenty-six people died, a majority of them *priistas*. On December 22, the father of one of the deceased *priistas* took his revenge at Acteal. The killers and victims were all indigenous, victims of internecine struggle. Zapatista sympathizers would argue that these local *priistas* were simply dupes of the party machine, acting against their ethnic interest, but events in Chiapas did not bear this view out. What Acteal revealed was a civil war in the highlands of Chiapas, brought on by scarce resources, population pressures, and militarization.

During the late 1990s the federal government poured $3.5 billion in federal aid into Chiapan indigenous communities that chose not to support the Zapatistas, improving living conditions for *priistas* and opponents alike in those villages. Schools, medical clinics, food, and agricultural aid had a dramatic impact on many highland communities, cutting off the rebel municipalities even further. The Zapatista leadership forbade their followers from accepting any of this aid, resulting in a gradual out-migration from the regions they controlled, as desperate villagers moved to areas where they could receive government aid. Outside the rebel territories, indigenous Chiapans voted en masse for the PRD in the 2000 gubernatorial elections, putting the sole party that supported the San Andrés Accords into power at the state level. Their political loyalty had not been purchased by PRI largesse in the late 1990s, and their decision to participate at the polls offered hope that real change might come through peaceful means.

When Mexicans turfed the PRI out of the presidency in Mexico's most democratic elections in history, they did so with no help from the EZLN. The Zapatistas refused to participate in the elections, and the vote in the regions they controlled would not be counted. The Zapatistas had little belief in the electoral process, especially in Chiapas, where local elites had tightly controlled elections for decades, doing whatever it took to ensure PRI victories. Imagine the surprise, then, when in August 2000 the people of Chiapas voted the PRD into power at the state level. The PRD election victory in 2000 was a triumph for democratic practices in the state, a triumph for many of the poor and dispossessed in the region, but was, in no uncertain terms, a loss for the Zapatistas. In a larger sense, it revealed that the Chiapas conflict had been reduced to a sideshow in Mexican politics.

Given the marginalization of the EZLN by 2000, Fox may not have been overly naïve to imagine that he could solve the Chiapas problem in fifteen minutes.[10] With barely 1,000 men under (largely obsolete) arms, the Zapatistas no longer represented any kind of military threat. Fox could thus begin to withdraw troops from the state just hours after he came into office, without risk to federal authority. A few days later he sent an Indian Rights Bill based on the San Andrés Accords to Congress. The bill would have modified the constitution to grant indigenous communities autonomy, allowing them to pass local laws, use customary practices for choosing their leaders, receive a bilingual education, and have access to news media. It also guaranteed indigenous peoples an "equitable" share of the national wealth. Encouraged by Fox's proposal, in March 2001 the EZLN held a two-week "March for Dignity" from Chiapas to Mexico City. Thousands cheered them along the 2,000-mile march, which ended with a demonstration in Mexico City attended by perhaps 100,000 people.

Any hope for a quick end to the rebellion evaporated when the PAN delegation in Congress walked out of the chamber in protest when the Zapatistas spoke. The opposition was led by Diego Fernández de Cevallos, a wealthy landowner who headed the PAN in

Congress. Fernández, the PAN, the PRI, and the Green Party chafed at any suggestion of autonomy, and on April 28 passed a much-watered-down version of the bill, which instead of granting autonomy designated indigenous communities as "subjects of public interest," and denied collective rights to land and resources.[11] PRD deputy Uuc-Kib Espadas called it a "bitter day for the nation," and on April 29 the EZLN formally withdrew from negotiations, declaring that the new law betrayed the spirit of the San Andrés Accords. Other critics argued that the law violated treaties signed by the Mexican government, especially Article 169 of the International Labor Organization, which guarantees indigenous peoples a right to their territories.

In its final form the Ley Indígena favored a view on resource rights that was more in keeping with Fox's Plan Puebla Panamá (PPP) than the San Andrés Accords, which would have allowed indigenous communities to make decisions about their resources according to customary practices. The PPP was the final element of Fox's fifteen-minute solution, a grand vision of economic development that would turn the poor indigenous peoples of the region into middle-class businessmen through a program that developed the unique array of natural resources in the region. Local organizations have generally opposed the PPP, because it both bypasses community decision-making practices concerning resources, and seems destined to put most local resources in the hands of the politically connected.

Authority over the development rights of the land in question is problematic in any case. Many of the communities in the areas with the most potential for oil and other resources are squatters, recent arrivals whose legitimate claim to the land could be contested, and in no case could be justified through reference to possession from "time immemorial." Yet if the PPP was truly intended to benefit indigenous communities, it is hard to understand why the Fox administration could not find an alternative plan that offered concrete rights and control to its supposed beneficiaries. Was it that the Fox administration did not trust indigenous communities to pursue their own interests, or that federal control would allow other parties to monopolize the benefits derived from development in the region? The former theory suggests that Fox is well meaning if paternalistic, but the latter is buttressed by a long history of everyday practice in Mexico.

Never to be left out of the fray, Subcomandante Marcos had his own response to the Fox development plan:

> We cannot trust someone who has displayed superficiality and ignorance by noting that the indigenous demands will be resolved with "vocho" [literally the Volkswagen Beetle; figuratively, access to material goods], TV and little shops ... At the end of the day, this plan is nothing other than an attempt to continue the ethnocide which, under different methods, neoliberalism in Mexico is carrying forward ... Your program of "disappearing an indigenous and creating a businessperson" will not be allowed on our soil. Here, and under many other Mexican skies, the indigenous self does not have to do only with blood and origin, but also with the vision of life, death, culture, land, history, the future.

Relatively few people in Mexico were listening by this point. The early impact of Marcos's appearances and declarations had waned into a curiosity even before the débâcle of the Ley Indígena. Chiapas saw continued violence, but the local PRD government was able to create at least some forums for open and legal dissent in the state. This only marginalized the Zapatistas further, so much so that when Fox visited the state in early 2005 he declared that the uprising was essentially over; that Chiapas was secure, governed by the rule of law, respect for the law, tranquility, and peace. He was echoed by the PRD governor of Chiapas, Pablo Salazar Mendiguchía, who commented that "Zapatismo as an armed option is a thing of the past." Fox's visit also served to highlight the efforts undertaken by the government to open free medical clinics, attend to the poor, and reduce illiteracy in the state, programs that have not been implemented in rebel territory.

The poverty of democracy

In the past quarter-century a host of individuals and organizations have worked tirelessly to create the web of organizations, institutions, and practices that constitute Mexican democracy. And yet Mexicans need more than a simple procedural democracy. Mexico is one of the most unequal societies in the Americas. Wages for working-class Mexicans have been stagnant or falling for decades.

Eighty-one percent of indigenous Mexicans, who comprise 10–15 percent of the population, live in poverty. Federal officials claim to be working on these problems, but they have spent many billions more in expanding the repressive capacities of the state in recent years than in fighting poverty. This tendency suggests that while Mexico has become a freer society, it has also become a more dangerous place for those who have not shared in the benefits of globalization.

Democracy in and of itself is a poor antidote to increasing inequality within global capitalism. One of the critical measures of democracy lies in examining not just participation but the actual benefits derived from participation. In Mexico, political elites encouraged popular participation in the democratic transition, but they resisted structural change from below. Official politics generally takes place within boundaries that reaffirm the goals articulated by technocrats within the PRI two decades ago. As Miguel Centeno observed in 1997, Fox represented democracy without macroeconomic change, and was exactly what the technocrats in the PRI had long desired.

Political openings have not generally translated into more liberty for Mexican workers and the poor. Even as they have gained an effective vote, workers are still represented by phantom unions, which negotiate contracts with no oversight from their rank and file. Labor laws written in the era of PRI hegemony continue to allow employers to negotiate secret contracts with local labor boards, without any participation from workers, who have no right to challenge the contract. Furthermore, their contract remains secret once negotiated. Once a workforce is represented by a CTM-affiliated union (certification can take place in secret, without the workers' knowledge), workers first need to decertify the union to which they belong before they can form a new union. This requires a public disavowal of the union in front of plant managers and union officials, often done amid a throng of thugs who beat and otherwise intimidate any opponents of the "official" union. It is thus not surprising that decertification efforts continue to fail, even as independent unions and union democracy movements have gained momentum.

Poor Mexicans also feel the incompleteness of Mexico's democratic transition. At the local level, in villages and neighborhoods, poor people work on things they can affect, and in areas where their results cannot be appropriated by the state. Active, aggressive efforts to provide services to poor neighborhoods, and movements to clean up living spaces, undercut domestic violence, expose police abuse and corruption, and change the quotidian conditions of life in poor neighborhoods represent the most important and direct method that poor people have had of participating in Mexico's new democracy.

Beyond the local level, poor people find their options severely restricted. Political parties generally do not represent their interests, and they are left to extra-institutional means to make their voices heard. A system based on patronage and connections within the PRI that used to provide millions of average Mexicans with an opportunity to share in the spoils of the system is gone, replaced only by a feeling that the working class has been abandoned. Since few institutional mechanisms have been created to empower poor people, they must exert pressure through non-institutional means. Among others, workers, students, peasants, community activists, and small businessmen continue to work in the ways they always have – mass protests, strikes, slow-downs at critical junctures. In the past these tactics worked by pressuring the president to make concessions. Today, the matter has become more complex. The president no longer has the power to meet their demands, and the protests often do not produce predictable results. Popular protests did put a stop to airport construction plans in Mexico City in 2002, and saved López Obrador in early 2005, but they are a poor substitute for actual participation. They are the kind of blunt instrument that risks undermining the interests of the protesters themselves.

Mexicans are less sympathetic to public disruptions than they were in an era when there were no democratic alternatives, and those who use mass demonstrations or violence to protest the oligarchical nature of Mexico's democracy risk being branded as throwbacks to another era. This fact was made dramatically clear during the eleven-month student strike at the UNAM, which began on April 20, 1999. A strike committee shut down the 300,000-student campus, erecting blockades and refusing administrators, police, and opponents any access to the campus. Their protest began over a plan by the government to impose tuition fees at the university, but after the government quickly capitulated, the strikers remained defiant because they believed the government intended to privatize the school. The *ultras*, as the most militant students were known, refused to end their occupation of the campus, held demonstrations throughout the city, and demanded wholesale changes at the university. Few Mexicans took their demands seriously, and the strike ended when 2,500 members of the PFP entered the campus and arrested the 600 remaining strikers on February 6, 2000.

The PFP invasion of the campus was a military takeover, and to the strikers it evoked images of 1968. To most Mexicans, however, it was long overdue. Even from the start, many Mexicans viewed the strike committee not as heroes, but as thugs, a view that was reinforced when striking students "defaced" a mural by David Siqueiros. A majority of their fellow students opposed the strike committee, repeatedly demanding that they end their occupation of the campus and allow classes to resume once the government conceded on tuition. Even in poor neighborhoods, where residents identified deeply with the defense of a free public education, the strikers lost sympathy as their intransigence seemed to threaten the survival of the university.

That the Mexican population for the most part was either indifferent or hostile to the strikers, and did not erupt in rage at the invasion of the school, was not a sign of apathy. To the contrary, this response, like the increasing indifference to the EZLN shared by millions of Mexicans, represents one of the fundamental but incomplete changes associated with democratization. The Mexican public may not have a great deal of faith in their processes or politicians, but neither does the public favor movements that do not appear to obey the democratic will. For the militant left, which could always count on the basic illegitimacy of the one-party state as a critical symbolic tool, this is a challenge that has not yet been resolved. Efforts to taint the three-party state with the condemnation once reserved for the one-party state have largely fallen on deaf ears. The strike committee became an anachronism when it ignored the popular will.

Epilogue: 2006

As this book was being written, Mexicans were preparing for the 2006 presidential elections. Historians write about the past in part because we fear predictions, and I will make no exception here. Instead, I hope to offer some observations about the trajectory of Mexican politics, given Mexico's recent past and regional trends. Fifteen years ago Latin American leftists had a great deal of reason to fear the future of globalization. Latin America was under siege from ideologues in the IMF and the World Bank, the edifices of the welfare state were collapsing throughout the region, and even old-style populists like the Peronists in Argentina had embraced neo-liberal economic reforms. Except in Cuba, which was then going through the worst economic crisis since the Revolution – people were in fact starving – the left was on the defensive everywhere in Latin America.

A decade and a half later, democratic elections have brought leftists to power in Chile, Brazil, Argentina, Uruguay, Venezuela, and Bolivia. A fiery Hugo Chávez openly defies the US, promises a "Bolivarian revolution," and regularly proclaims the deficiencies of capitalism. Riding high on record oil prices, Chávez has provided oil at cut rates to his fellow travelers, and recently launched a regional television network to counter the influence of the behemoth to the north. To be fair, he still relies on oil sales to the US to finance his revolution, and most of his leftist colleagues throughout the region have done little to remedy the inequality created by neo-liberal globalization (in fact, most support free trade), but for the left in and around Latin America these are hopeful times.

Some foreigners see Andrés Manuel López Obrador as a figure not unlike Chávez, an idealist who would use Mexico's considerable oil wealth to rectify the injustices of a quarter-century of reform. This is a mistaken view, a misapprehension of both López Obrador and of the Mexican political landscape. López Obrador is a hero to many for his social programs, development efforts, populist rhetoric, and political biography (he once moved his family to a community of Chontal Indians in order to initiate a series of public works campaigns in the village, and while in the village lived in a shack with a dirt floor), but in his campaign for the presidency he situated himself as a "centrist," and he has worked closely with the business sector to restore the core of the city.[12]

These tendencies should make us align López Obrador more closely with the President of Brazil, Luiz Inácio "Lula" da Silva, than with Hugo Chávez. Whereas in Venezuela the former paratrooper turned coup leader turned president has governed through a highly polarizing style, building close ties with Cuba, vilifying the oligarchy and global capitalism, Lula has been constrained in a way that a leftist president in Mexico would also likely be. The regional, economic, and political heterogeneity of Mexico militates against a Venezuelan-style future. This is not to say that Chávez (and for that matter Castro) does not have supporters in Mexico, but rather that Mexico would probably not be a good fit for Chávez's political style. The sheer momentum of the democratizing process has made old-style populism seem anachronistic to a significant percentage of Mexicans. More than this, the three principal parties in Mexico have strong and distinct regional bases, making it unlikely that someone like Chávez could find a national following based on his polarizing rhetoric and tendencies.

The PAN and PRI would face similar limitations if their candidates were to win the 2006 elections. A PAN led by Felipe Calderón (Calderón, a native of Michoacán and Fox's former energy minister, won the nomination over Santiago Creel in part due to the scandal over the gambling licenses), could be easily blocked in Congress by shifting coalitions of PRI and PRD law-makers. Roberto Madrazo's PRI would face the same prospects, and would also be challenged by thousands of NGOs whose demands for transparency could be embarrassing and disastrous for his party. Beyond this, Madrazo, Calderón, and López Obrador face severe critics in their own parties, limiting their capacity to act as autocrats.[13]

When 750,000 protesters took to the streets of Mexico City in March 2005, they did so as much to defend the democratic process as they did to defend López Obrador. They made the entire process against López Obrador look tawdry, embarrassing the Mexican president not just at home but across the globe. Their voices represent the clearest possible evidence that Mexico's future presidents will not govern Mexico in the fashion in which PRI presidents did for seven decades. This, then, represents one of the central paradoxes of globalization in Mexico. Globalization has been characterized by growing inequality and a deeply problematic model of economic development. It has also underpinned the emergence of a vibrant civic and political life.

Notes

1 Why 1989?

1 Popular was a catch-all sector, drawing largely from the petite bourgeoisie.

2 These included high tariffs, direct import controls, government restrictions on foreign direct investment, tax concessions for manufacturing and subsidies, and exchange rate controls to promote importation of large-scale machinery and equipment.

3 At 12.5 to the dollar from the 1950s until 1975.

4 Agriculture continued to employ 40 percent of the working population into the 1970s, when it produced only 10 percent of GDP.

5 A corollary of this was Mexico's highly regressive tax code. By the late 1960s labor's share of income tax receipts to the government was over 75 percent.

6 Unless otherwise noted, all amounts are in US dollars.

7 Echeverría also increased the money supply, and expanded the rural electrical grid, expanded the Compañía Nacional de Subsistencias Populares (CONASUPO) to regulate the market for basic commodities, increase income for small farmers, and ensure availability of basic goods to low-income consumers. Nearly 20 percent of the budget was targeted at rural development during his presidency. He also stepped up repression of political dissidents.

8 100,000 acres in Sonora were redistributed from large landowners to peasants.

9 He acquired this wealth through a series of rackets, which included corruption, arms dealing, and extortion. Though it was never proven, he was also allegedly involved in the drug trade. He was convicted in 1986 and released from jail in 1992.

10 When, in the aftermath, de la Madrid did deign to appear for the inauguration of new public housing built by the government for earthquake victims, critics were quick to point out that it was the Red Cross and international relief agencies, not the Mexican government, which had built the housing. What was the Mexican contribution? They had taken down the Red Cross banner moments before the event.

2 Salinastroika

1 The term refers to the six-year period of Mexican presidential administrations. There is no re-election in Mexico for any elected politician. This

measure was adopted in the 1917 constitution (along with earlier ones) in an effort to prevent dictatorships.

2 Prior to the reform 100 percent of imports required licenses. As a result of their reforms just 9 percent of imports needed licenses.

3 The Border Industrialization Program, was launched to help deal with unemployment along the border in the aftermath of the termination of the Bracero Program. Under this program machinery, equipment, and components were imported to Mexico duty free in a 20-kilometer strip along the border. The stipulation was that everything imported would then be exported. The plants are popularly known as *maquilas*, or *maquiladoras*. See Chapter 5.

4 This was the title of Salinas's own memoir of his presidency.

5 These programs had only ever provided benefits to about half of Mexican workers.

6 The *Concordancia* that Salinas signed with the pope, which re-established relations with Rome for the first time since the revolution, signaled that religious schools and foreign priests were secure.

7 It was based on a 1994 World Bank proposal.

8 This too was in part based on World Bank recommendations.

9 It was spread much more thinly than earlier programs, because it subsidized subsistence producers as well as commercial growers.

10 His cabinet was typical of this tendency. It was composed of a combination of young technocrats with advanced degrees from US universities (Yale, Harvard, MIT, Northwestern, Stanford, Penn) and old-style politicos like Carlos Hank González, a legendary and legendarily corrupt politician. Salinas also appointed Fernando Gutiérrez Barrios, the long-time chief of the Federal Security Agency, and intellectual architect of the massacre at Tlatelolco, as interior minister.

11 The first elections held in Mexico under the new rules were held on August 18, 1991. The contests saw some problems, but were easily the most transparent in Mexican history. The final tally gave 61.5 percent and 320 deputies to the PRI, 17.7 percent and eighty-nine seats to the PAN, and only 8.2 percent of the vote to the PRD.

12 4.2 percent in 1989, followed by 5.1, 4.2, 3.6, 2.0, and 4.5 percent in 1994.

3 Nineteen ninety-four

1 They took Altamirano, Chanal, Huistán, Las Magaritas, Oxchuc, and Ocosingo, along with San Cristóbal de las Casas.

2 <www.actlab.utexas.edu/~zapatistas/auto.html>.

3 <www.geocities.com/CapitolHill/1364/cpage1.htm>

4 <www.chiapaslink.ukgateway.net/ch1.html>

5 <www.chiapaslink.ukgateway.net/ch1.html>

6 Speedy Gonzalez is an American cartoon figure, often criticized as a racist caricature of Mexicans. Until recently the EZLN web site <www.ezln.org> was run by a webmaster at UC-Santa Cruz, who claimed that its content was approved by the EZLN. The site maintains pages in English, Spanish, French, and Portuguese. It is connected to more than fifty other supporting sites, from places as varied as Italy, Spain, Russia, Canada, Australia, Ireland, the UK, and the US.

7 While they explicitly rejected racism, their modernizing ethos and patronizing approach to indigenous communities often produced a similar effect. The INI's assimilationist mandate in this era also precluded serious consideration of an indigenous right to self-determination, though some local officials did endeavor to promote pluralism.

8 It was named after the site where, in 1914, the original Zapatistas participated in a constitutional convention.

9 Nestor García Canclini (1995) argues that cultures in this sense can be simultaneously traditional and modern.

10 Indigenous movements also became increasingly militant over this period. The First Continental Meeting of *pueblos indios* drafted a "Declaration of Quito" in August 1990, in which self-determination was the key demand. It called for indigenous communities to have a right to practice customary law, control their own territories, including natural resources, subsoil, and airspace, and framed this in a notion that indigenous communities will preserve the ecosystem.

11 The meetings were overseen by Bishop Samuel Ruiz García.

12 Posada was killed at the Guadalajara airport on May 24, 1993. He was widely admired for his energetic attacks on political corruption and the impunity of organized crime figures. His death was officially explained as a case of mistaken identity, but there were rumors that he was killed as he tried to negotiate an immunity agreement with Pablo Escobar on behalf of the Mexican government. In March 1994 the chairman of Mexico's largest bank, Alfredo Harp Helú, was kidnapped, setting off a wave of kidnappings among Mexico's elites. He was released after three months and a ransom of several million dollars.

4 The last days of the PRI?

1 His father's 1969 death is shrouded in rumors, in part because he had been an early advocate of democratization.

2 He was rumored to take 10 percent off the top as a bribe in all public contracts he had a hand in.

3 As evidence mounted that he had embezzled $45 million as mayor of the Federal District, Oscar Espinosa – former mayor of the Federal District, and finance chairman of Zedillo's campaign – resigned as Secretary of Tourism in 2000 and went into hiding. In 2003 he was sentenced to four years in jail and ordered to pay a fine of $50 million.

4 In the divorce, allegations of homosexuality were made. He also

suggested that political conflicts between the men and the political ambitions of Ruiz Massieu motivated the murder.

5 French officials have charged him with money laundering.

6 Villanueva is also accused of taking bribes to manipulate the privatization of Cancún's garbage and water systems, along with selling permissions to build hotels in the region.

7 In one horrifying massacre, nineteen men, women, and children were found murdered on September 17, 1998 in Ensenada.

8 The Civic Alliance was the umbrella organization for NGOs committed to democracy and human rights. They also oversaw the 1994 election. See Chapter 1.

9 The Confederation of Mexican Workers. See Chapter 1.

10 In Huejotzingo, Puebla, in May 1996, Zedillo forced the PRI mayor to resign and give the office to the PAN.

11 More broadly, Fox did best among the young, where he won 50 percent of the vote. Sixty percent of those with college degrees voted for him, along with 59 percent of students. The PRI did best among those with no schooling (46 percent), as did Cárdenas, who won 21 percent of the vote among those with no schooling. Forty-two percent of those over sixty voted for Labastida, compared to 35 percent for Fox, and 22 percent for Cárdenas.

5 Border crossings in an age of terror

1 Migrants were required to return to Mexico at the end of their contracts.

2 The act was reformed in 1965, 1976, 1978, and 1980.

3 These numbers reflect the fact that migrants often returned home twice or more per year. The actual number of migrants is a fraction of the total.

4 The Border Patrol now has around 11,000 officers.

5 A coordinated effort to undermine smuggling efforts in the region led to the arrest of 48,000 Mexicans.

6 The total population of Mexican origin in the US is now more than 23 million.

7 Cinco de Mayo (the fifth of May) celebrates the victory of Mexican forces over the French at the battle of Puebla, in 1862. There are large celebrations in several US cities.

8 Latino denotes all US citizens of Latin American ancestry.

9 One recent study suggests that as much as half of the money sent as remittances to Mexico does not go to poor families, but is sent in payment for goods imported by small businesses (such as hard-to-find delicacies imported from Mexico by bodegas in Los Angeles). Remittances also pay for smugglers to bring human cargoes into the US, and include donations from American churches to their Mexican counterparts. It is also possible

that some of the remittances are laundered profits from the drug trade, though the small amounts of individual payments (averaging less than $400) suggest otherwise. At its most conservative, this might mean that fewer than 7 percent of poor households actually receive remittances. More liberal estimates suggest that 17 percent of Mexicans receive remittances. Neither of these figures accounts for the multiplier effect of remittances.

10 Two-thirds of Mexico's diplomatic service is also engaged in the US. After 2000 a growing number of states would also open offices there.

11 They shared bonhomie rooted in anti-intellectualism, deep religious faith, and an affinity for the ranching ethos. Both were also former businessmen (though Bush's record of failure contrasts with Fox's successes), and shared a commitment to cutting through bureaucratic malaise and pursuing "common sense" solutions to social and economic problems.

12 Alarmed by the possibility that voters in other states might not respond like Californians, Republicans in Congress are currently undertaking efforts to force states to deny drivers' licenses to undocumented migrants.

13 Their efforts have stalled in the courts, but may be revived in the future.

14 At the same time the Border Patrol assigned 500 more agents to Arizona.

15 Castro was angry that Fox had criticized Castro's human rights record.

16 Since Fox took office ninety soldiers and sixty-five AFI agents have also been killed in drug-related violence.

17 This is a vulgar slang term referring to people from Mexico City.

18 Exasperated by federal inaction, in June 2005 residents of Baja California held a March for Peace.

6 A decade of NAFTA

1 Zedillo reduced public spending by 10 percent in real terms, increased VAT from 10 to 15 percent, and raised prices for fuel, electricity, and social services.

2 Mexico now sends 90 percent of its exports to the US, up from 70 percent in 1994. This helped Mexico overtake Japan as the country's second most important trading partner.

3 Under NAFTA almost 70 percent of exports have consisted of car and car parts (the automobile industry now accounts for 15 percent of GDP), electric goods and electronics, and machinery.

4 Income inequality, which declined between 1963 and 1980, has grown steadily since 1980 (with only a brief respite in 1994–96). The top 10 percent of the population now accounts for 35 percent of income, while the bottom 40 percent earns 13.3 percent.

5 In early 2005 the SEC charged Ricardo B. Salinas Pliego, chairman

of TV Azteca, with fraud. It seems that Salinas sold a debt from Unefon (which he owned) to Codisco (in which he had an undisclosed interest) at a deep discount in 2003, and then resold the debt to Unefon at full price in a deal that netted him $109 million. Investors in his companies were not informed of the transactions or Salinas's ties to Codisco until his New York law firm resigned in protest in late 2003. Charges are also pending in Mexico, and Mexican regulators have already fined Salinas $2.3 million for violations of securities laws, though he claims that these charges are simply an effort to silence TV Azteca's investigations into improprieties in the 1990s bank bail-out. Salinas has used his power as owner of TV Azteca to launch a vigorous public defense, and has called for criminal charges against top government officials.

6 Currently the peso trades at around eleven to the dollar. By comparison, the US president earns $400,000 per year, congressmen earn $158,000 per year, and the Chief Justice of the Supreme Court earns a salary of $202,000 per year. Members of the British Parliament earn $101,000 (£57,485).

7 Other significant categories of employment include merchants, sellers, artisans, and office personnel. Women today also make up 25 percent of *ejidatarios* (up from 1.3 percent in 1970).

8 The illiteracy rate among women has also fallen from nearly 30 percent to 11.3 percent. In 1970 only 4.9 percent of women received a post-secondary education, whereas today 26.4 percent do. Divorced women have increased from 2.6 percent of the population to 5 percent, and the number of female-headed households has increased from 1,705,234 in 1970 to 4,597,335. The economic and political power offered by these changes may be the most important avenue available for women. In 2000 women won 20 percent of elected offices nationwide, and today there are twenty-eight women in the 128-seat Senate, and 117 women in the 500-seat Chamber of Deputies. There is one female justice in the Supreme Court and one woman in the cabinet (along with two in the extended cabinet).

9 The term refers to plots of land, ranging from tiny *ejidos* to vast ranches.

10 The results were reported in *La Jornada*, and on a least a dozen Latin American websites. See, for example, <http://uruguay.indymedia.org/news/2005/07/36694.php?theme=default>, <http://forajidos.org/rebelion/modules/news/index.php?storytopic=0&start=15>, and <www.consumidoresint.cl/noticias2005.asp?anho=2005&mes=Mayo>.

11 Thirty-three million Mexicans have funds in fifteen different AFORES, named for the Administradora de Fondos del Retiro (created in 1997). The program has been a boon for the state, as the funds have invested over $7 billion in public works projects (including the new terminal for Mexico City's airport), but the new system has proved to have much higher overheads than the old system. Contemporary commissions are more than double the old service charges. On top of this, the government continues to contract significant debts to pay the pensions still owed

to people under the old system, a cost that will amount to between 1 and 1.5 percent of GNP over the next sixty years.

12 The wide variation is due to the fact that poverty can be measured in a number of different ways, producing dramatically different results.

13 PRONASOL collapsed in the financial crisis of 1995, when government spending as a whole was reduced by 15 percent. Under Zedillo, spending on social welfare fell to 0.4 percent of GNP in 1996, 0.3 per cent in 1997, and 0.2 percent in 1998.

14 A *corrido* is a popular type of ballad in Mexico.

15 In an effort to appease public outrage, some provisions to help small debtors were added to the rescue package, but these provisions were mostly cosmetic.

16 In 2005 the government agreed to allow PEMEX to keep more earnings, but these resources may not be enough to cover the company's needs.

17 The PPP includes plans for colonization, deregulation, social programs, public works, fiscal incentives, intensive plantations, monocrops, commercial service corridors, assembly plants, tourism, and bioprospecting.

18 Mexico lags behind its competitors in public education. Less than 60 percent complete their six-year primary education, and less than 3 percent graduate from university.

7 Conclusion

1 Critics derided his advisors as a "Montessori" cabinet because of their inability to create a coherent set of policies.

2 Between 1934 and 1997, 86.7 percent of Mexico's legislators served a single three-year term.

3 Mexico's National Commission for Human Rights (CNDH) defines human rights according to three categories. The first includes political and civic human rights, defined as "classic" liberties. These include the right to life, liberty, and juridical security for all, without regard to race, color, language, social or economic position, prohibitions against slavery and servitude, freedom from torture and cruel, degrading, and unusual punishment, freedom from arbitrary detention and harassment, the right to move freely and live where one chooses, the right to a nationality, the right to asylum, freedom to marry whomever one chooses and over the choice of procreation, freedom of thought and religion, of expression, and of peaceful association. The other categories of rights pursued by the CNDH include social and economic rights (including work, social security, education, health, and others), and the rights associated with the self-determination of minority groups.

4 Currently about five thousand military personnel are on loan to the PFP.

5 This figure included 1,703 complaints of arbitrary detention.

6 Also in October 2003 the Senate created a commission to oversee the investigation.

7 Fox's reform is modeled on the system of criminal justice in the US, and was drawn up with collaboration from US officials (USAID) and advice from the UN Commission on Human Rights.

8 The PRI always used local power brokers (*caciques*) to bring out indigenous voters on election day, on the assumption that they could use a variety of forms of soft and hard compulsion to ensure that indigenous Mexicans voted for the party.

9 Mexico's National Commission for the Development of Indian Peoples estimates that there are 12 million indigenous people in Mexico, of whom more than 6 million speak one of 100 indigenous languages.

10 He declared this during the campaign.

11 Called the Ley de Derechos y Cultura Indígenas, it passed by 386 votes to 60. In the following months enough states ratified the bill in order to make it a constitutional amendment. It was rejected by the eleven states that comprise most of the indigenous population of Mexico.

12 He also does not escape criticism that he has subverted democratic processes in his own party, blocked the enforcement of freedom of information laws, and has overseen some fairly irresponsible projects as mayor. His refusal to legalize gay unions in the city has also drawn the ire of gay rights activists.

13 The democratic wing of the party is deeply critical of Madrazo, and tried to find another candidate for 2006. Madrazo has resurrected the PRI, though questions remain as to whether the PRI he has resurrected would respect the democratic process. This has been particularly evident in a series of recent elections in Oaxaca and Veracruz, where candidates supported by Madrazo used illegal campaign funds and political assassinations to win office. Some of his closest allies, including Jorge Hank Rhon, former mayor of Tijuana, are suspected of laundering drug money. Opponents of Madrazo within the PRI, led by Arturo Montiel of Mexico, Natividad Gonzalez of Nuevo Léon, and Eduardo Bours of Sonora, have formed a coalition called Todos Unidos Contra Madrazo (TUCOM). They are particularly alarmed at charges of corruption and authoritarianism. Montiel was Madrazo's primary opponent for the nomination, but dropped out of the race in mid-October 2005 in the midst of a financial scandal.

Suggestions for further reading

General

The following texts endeavor to assess the impact of the political and economic transformations that Mexico has undergone in recent years.

Bonfil Batalla, G. (1996) *México Profundo: Reclaiming a Civilization*, Austin: University of Texas Press.

Fuentes, C. (1997) *A New Time for Mexico*, Berkeley: University of California Press.

García Canclini, N. (1999) *La globalización imaginada*, Mexico: Paidós.

Gutmann, M. C. (2002) *The Romance of Democracy: Compliant Defiance in Contemporary Mexico*, Berkeley: University of California Press.

Hellman, J. A. (1994) *Mexican Lives*, New York: New Press.

Lomnitz, C. (2001) *Deep Mexico, Silent Mexico: An Anthropology of Nationalism*, Minneapolis: University of Minnesota Press.

Monsiváis, C. (1997) *Mexican Postcards*, London: Verso.

Preston, J. and S. Dillon (2004) *Opening Mexico: The Making of a Democracy*, New York: Farrar, Straus & Giroux.

Historical background

Changes in the global economy and international power structures have long had a significant impact in Mexico, though Mexicans have always dealt with larger processes on their own terms. Some important sources for the historical background to recent changes are listed below.

Bethell, L. (ed.) (1991) *Mexico Since Independence*, Cambridge: Cambridge University Press.

Brading, D. A. (1993) *The First America: The Spanish Monarchy, Creole Patriots and the Liberal State 1492–1866*, Cambridge, Cambridge University Press.

Davis, D. E. (1994) *Urban Leviathan: Mexico City in the Twentieth Century*, Philadelphia, PA: Temple University Press.

Joseph, G. and D. Nugent (eds) (1994) *Everyday Forms of State Formation: Revolution and the Negotiation of Rule in Modern Mexico*, Durham, NC: Duke University Press.

Knight, A. (1986) *The Mexican Revolution*, 2 vols, Cambridge: Cambridge University Press.

Krauze, E. (1997) *Mexico: Biography of Power: A History of Modern Mexico, 1810–1996*, New York: HarperCollins.

Middlebrook, K. J. (1995) *The Paradox of Revolution: Labor, the State, and Authoritarianism in Mexico*. Baltimore, MD: Johns Hopkins University Press.

Paz, O. (1985) *The Labyrinth of Solitude: The Other Mexico, Return to the Labyrinth of Solitude, Mexico and the United States, the Philanthropic Ogre*, New York: Grove Press.

Poniatowska, E. (1971) *La noche de Tlatelolco*, Mexico: Era.

— (1988) *Nothing, Nobody: The Voices of the Mexico City Earthquake*, Philadelphia, PA: Temple University Press.

Rubin, J. W. (1997) *Decentering the Regime: Ethnicity, Radicalism, and Democracy in Juchitan, Mexico*, Durham, NC: Duke University Press.

Smith, P. H. (1979) *Labyrinths of Power: Political Recruitment in Twentieth-century Mexico*, Princeton, NJ: Princeton University Press.

Tutino, J. (1986) *From Insurrection to Revolution in Mexico: Social Bases of Agrarian Violence, 1750–1940*, Princeton, NJ: Princeton University Press.

Zolov, E. (1999) *Refried Elvis: The Rise of the Mexican Counterculture*, Berkeley: University of California Press.

Economic reform

The impacts of Mexico's economic reforms since the mid-1980s remain disputed. Data available from the Instituto Nacional de Estadísticas, Geografía e Informática (<www.inegi.gob.mx/inegi/>) can be interpreted in a variety of ways, and many studies of the Mexican economy even disagree on basic statistical data. The following texts embody some of those disagreements.

Babb, S. (2004) *Managing Mexico: Economists from Nationalism to Neoliberalism*, Princeton, NJ: Princeton University Press.

Edwards, S. and M. Naím (eds) (1997) *Mexico, 1994: Anatomy of an Emerging-market Crash*, New York: Carnegie Endowment for International Peace.

Krause, E. (1999) *El sexenio de Carlos Salinas*, Mexico: Clío.

Lustig, N. (1998) *Mexico: The Remaking of an Economy*, Washington, DC: Brookings Institution Press.

Middlebrook, K. J. and E. Zepeda (2003) *Confronting Development: Assessing Mexico's Economic and Social Policy Challenges*, Stanford, CA: Stanford University Press.

Office of the United States Trade Representative and Related Entities (n.d.) *Study on the Operation and Effect of the North American Free Trade Agreement*, <www.sice.oas.org/geograph/north/nafreptc.asp>.

Otero, G. (ed.) (2004) *Mexico in Transition: Neoliberal Globalism, the State, and Civil Society*, London: Zed Books.

Salinas de Gortari, C. (2000) *México: un paso difícil a la modernidad*, Barcelona : Plaza & Janés Editores.

US–Mexican relations

Several issues continue to define US–Mexican relations. These include economic integration, migration, and the drug trade. Statistics on each are widely available from government agencies, though since the latter two flows are not legally sanctioned, information tends to be somewhat speculative. Migration and the drug trade are also subject to wild rumors on the Web, and demagoguery in both countries. Some useful sources are listed below.

Andreas, P. (2001) *Border Games: Policing the US–Mexico Divide*, Ithaca, NY: Cornell University Press.

Castañeda, J. G. (1995) *The Mexican Shock: Its Meaning for the US*, New York: New Press.

Durand, J., D. S. Massey and E. A. Parrado (n.d.) "The new era of Mexican migration to the United States," <www.indiana.edu/~jah/mexico/jdurand.html>.

Durand, J., D. S. Massey and R. Zenteno (2001), "Mexican immigration to the United States: continuities and changes," *Latin American Research Review*, 36(1): 107–27.

Martínez, R. (2001) *Crossing Over: A Mexican Family on the Migrant Trail*, New York: Picador.

Massey, D. (2003) *Beyond Smoke and Mirrors: Mexican Immigration in an Era of Economic Integration*, New York: Russell Sage.

Massey, D. S. and C. Capoferro (2004) "Measuring undocumented migration," *International Migration Review*, 38: 1075–102.

Mazza, J. (2001) *Don't Disturb the Neighbors. The United States and Democracy in Mexico, 1980–1995*, New York: Routledge.

Mexican Migration Project (n.d.) <http://mmp.opr.princeton.edu/>.

Nevins, J. (2001) *Operation Gatekeeper: The Rise of the "Illegal Alien" and the Remaking of the US–Mexico Boundary*, New York: Routledge.

Oppenheimer, A. (1996) *Bordering on Chaos: Guerrillas, Stockbrokers, Politicians, and Mexico's Road to Prosperity*, New York: Little, Brown.

Rodriguez-Scott, E. (2002) "Patterns of Mexican migration to the United States," Paper prepared for delivery at the 82nd annual meeting of the Southwestern Social Science Association, New Orleans, LA, March 27–30.

Urrea, L. A. (1993) *Across the Wire: Life and Hard Times on the Mexican Border*, New York: Anchor.

Wood, A. G. (2004) *On the Border: Society and Culture Between the United States and Mexico,* Wilmington: Scholarly Resources.

Democratization and human rights

Democratization is a multi-faceted process in Mexico. Among other issues, the texts listed below consider the changing nature of the PRI, the rise of opposition parties, institutional democracy, and the changing regime of human rights in Mexico. Since many of these issues are tied to ongoing processes, it is sometimes easiest to find the most current information on these issues through the websites of a variety of official and non-governmental organizations. The US State Department issues detailed analyses of human rights in Mexico on an annual basis (<www.state.gov/g/drl/hr/>), as does the Comisión Nacional de Derechos Humanos in Mexico (<www.cndh.org.mx/>). The UN, Amnesty International (<http://web.amnesty.org/pages/hrd-index-eng>), America's Watch, Human Rights Watch (<http://hrw.org/doc?t=americas&c=mexico>) and the Interhemispheric Resource Center (<www.irc-online.org>) also release regular reports on democracy and human rights in Mexico.

Bruhn, K. (1997) *Taking on Goliath: The Emergence of a New Left Party and the Struggle for Democracy in Mexico*, University Park, PA: Pennsylvania State University Press.

Camp, R. A. (2002a) *Politics in Mexico: The Democratic Transformation*, Oxford: Oxford University Press.

— (2002b) *Mexico's Mandarins: Crafting a Power Elite for the Twenty-first Century*, Berkeley: University of California Press.

Castañeda, J. G. (2000) *Perpetuating Power: How Mexican Presidents were Chosen*, New York: New Press.

Centeno, M. A. (1997) *Democracy within Reason: Technocratic Revolution in Mexico*, University Park, PA: Pennsylvania State University Press.

Crandall, R., G. Paz and R. Roett (eds) (2005) *Mexico's Democracy at Work: Political and Economic Dynamics*, Boulder, CO: Lynne Rienner.

Domínguez, J. I. and C. Lawson (eds) (2004) *Mexico's Pivotal Democratic Election: Candidates, Voters, and the Presidential Campaign of 2000*, Stanford, CA: Stanford University Press.

Guerrero Rosas, E. (2004) *Los demonios de la transición? Cómo exorcizarlos?*, Mexico: Diana.

Levy, D. C., K. Bruhn with E. Zebadúa (2001) *Mexico: The Struggle for Democratic Development*, Berkeley: University of California Press.

Rubio, L. and S. Kaufman Purcell (2003) *Mexico Under Fox*, Boulder, CO: Lynne Rienner.

Scherer García, J. and C. Monsiváis (2003) *Tiempo de saber. Prensa y poder en México*, Mexico: Aguilar.

Schmidt, S. (2003) *Los grandes problemas nacionales. Versión siglo xxi*, Mexico: Aguilar.

Semo, E. (2004) *La búsqueda. 2. La izquierda y el fin del régimen de partido de estado (1994–2000)*, Mexico: Oceano.

Shirk, D. A. (2005) *Mexico's New Politics: The PAN and Democratic Change*, Boulder, CO: Lynne Rienner.

Tulchin, J. S. and A. D. Selee (eds) (2002) *Mexico's Politics and Society in Transition*, Boulder, CO: Lynne Rienner.

The Zapatista rebellion and indigenous rights

There are many sources about the Zapatistas on the Web. Those that are devoted to the EZLN's declarations are the most useful. Those that make generalizations about the practices and impact of the Zapatistas on a national and international level tend to be fanciful. Some of the more carefully considered analyses of the rebellion and indigenous rights are listed below.

Collier, G. A. with E. L. Quaratiello (1999) *Basta! Land and the Zapatista Rebellion in Chiapas*, Oakland, CA: Food First Books.

Díaz Polanco, H. (1997) *Indigenous Peoples in Latin America: The Quest for Self-determination*, Boulder, CO: Westview.

García Canclini, N. (1995) *Hybrid Cultures: Strategies for Entering and Leaving Modernity*, Minneapolis: University of Minnesota Press.

Harvey, N. (1998) *The Chiapas Rebellion: The Struggle for Land and Democracy*, Durham, NC: Duke University Press.

Nash, J. C. (2001) *Mayan Visions: The Quest for Autonomy in the Age of Globalization*, New York: Routledge.

Ponce de León, J. (ed.) (2001) *Our World is Our Weapon: Selected Writings, Subcomandante Insurgente Marcos*, New York: Seven Stories Press.

Stephen, L. (2002) *Zapata Lives! Histories and Cultural Politics in Southern Mexico*, Berkeley: University of California Press.

Viquiera, J. P. and W. Sonnleitner (eds) (2000) *Democracia en tierras indígenas. Las elecciones en los altos de Chiapas (1991–1998)*, Mexico: CIESAS.

Warren, K. B. (1998) *Indigenous Movements and Their Critics: Pan-Maya Activism in Guatemala*, Princeton, NJ: Princeton University Press.

Womack, J., Jr. (ed.) (1999) *Rebellion in Chiapas: An Historical Reader*, New York: New Press.

Current news

Spanish readers can follow developing events in Mexico through a series of online publications. Major newspapers, including *La Jornada*, *El Universal* and *Reforma* can be read online, along with *Nexos* and *Proceso*. English readers can find information about Mexico in the NACLA Report on the Americas, on the websites of various human rights organizations, and in a variety of subject-oriented discussion groups. Major newspapers including the *New York Times*, the *Miami Herald* and the *Los Angeles Times* report regularly on Mexico.

Index